Cite It
Right

The SourceAid Guide to Citation, Research, and Avoiding Plagiarism

Co-Authors:

Tom Fox
Julia Johns
Sarah Keller

SourceAid, LLC   Osterville ◆ MA

Cite It Right
© 2007 by SourceAid, LLC.

First edition 2005
Second edition 2006
Third edition 2007

Published by SourceAid, LLC
P.O. Box 430, Osterville, Massachusetts 02655

If updated of information becomes available it will be provided on http://www.citeitright.com/.

For information, please contact by mail (see publisher address) or e-mail info@sourceaid.com.

ISBN 978-0-9771957-1-8 (SC)

Printed in the United States of America

Table of Contents

Preface

Writing a quality research paper can be a difficult task, one that requires hours of preparation, writing, and revising. At the same time, writing a thorough and thoughtful research paper is a truly exciting opportunity, one that gives researchers the chance to engage meaningfully with the distinguished work of others in their fields; writing is the vehicle through which researchers acquire and exercise their own voice, articulating their thoughts and ideas to the ongoing dialogue of academic exploration and discovery. This book is designed to help researchers navigate through the research and writing process.

The first portion of *Cite It Right* is a comprehensive research and writing guide. The research chapter walks you through the major steps in researching, from choosing your topic and gathering credible research materials to keeping track of your sources. The writing chapter highlights the key components of a quality paper, explaining how to develop strong topics, thesis statements, and body paragraphs, while offering ways to organize ideas to optimize your paper's argument.

The second section of this book is a simplified compilation of the citation formats in the four major writing styles (MLA, APA, CMS, and CSE). With its dedication to academic integrity and the elimination of plagiarism within academic communities, SourceAid saw the need for a more student-friendly research and citation handbook for students working in the major disciplines.

This citation manual is the natural extension of SourceAid.com's popular citation software, making comprehensive citation guidelines available to students even when they cannot access a computer.

General Advice Before You Get Started

Before you move forward into the research and writing process, there are a number of things that you should keep in mind.

- Plan ahead.

  Allocate your time adequately between each step in the research process. Choosing your sources wisely is just as important as developing quality insights and proofreading.

- Begin researching with a clear idea of your paper's purpose.

  It is often helpful to write a rough thesis statement before you start your research to keep you on track. Write down your own ideas before and during your research to avoid losing them in the midst of all the established scholarship that you will be researching. Documenting how each source contributes to your thesis in an annotated bibliography will help you focus on your claim.

- Be aware of all of the research assignment guidelines.

  Check to see if you are required to incorporate a certain number of sources into your writing and whether you are supposed to refer to a particular number of books or websites. Also pay close attention to assignment details such as page length, writing style, and the instructor's personal formatting preferences.

- Learn how to use the library to your advantage.

  You should understand the library's catalog system and how the books are arranged. Ask the librarians for assistance if you need help finding material. Librarians can show you reference materials that you might not find on your own.

- Skim potential sources.

  Ensure that materials are right for your thesis before checking them out of the library. It would be a shame to carry home ten books when only three or four of them have substantive content for your thesis claim.

- Question what you read.

  When reading other researchers' analytical essays, challenge their arguments to discover potential points to investigate and discuss in your paper. Think about other writers' logic, consider their arguments, and jot down your own reactions.

- Take accurate notes from your sources and record their citation information during your research.

  Attribute ideas and quotations to their rightful author and source using the writing style that your teacher or discipline requires. Begin creating your working bibliography immediately on SourceAid.com or create a working bibliography by hand by following the citation formats in this book.

1   Writing Ethics

This chapter explores the ethical dimensions of writing and researching. It focuses on source citation fundamentals and reiterates the negative consequences of plagiarism with examples of plagiarizers in the news.

Plagiarism Defined

A writer plagiarizes when he or she presents another writer's unique work as a product of his or her own knowledge or imagination.

Plagiarism occurs when an author fails to do any of the following tasks:

- Include required in-text citations or notes

- Provide a complete reference list

- Cite accurately

Plagiarism: A Contemporary Issue

Plagiarism is on the rise, and its consequences are becoming more drastic. In today's Web Era, plagiarism is common because it is easy for a writer to copy and paste others' ideas from the Internet, and difficult to properly document sources. Because plagiarism poses such an obvious threat to genuine learning, educators do not take plagiarism offenses lightly. It is increasingly common for colleges to rescind acceptance letters or deny graduation rights if they discover students plagiarized in the past or violated their academic integrity policies. Despite these disciplinary measures, some students in today's high-pressure culture will do anything to secure a diploma from a reputable institution and the well-paying job it ensures, even at the cost of their own academic integrity.

As you will see in the real life stories in the next section about citing sources, plagiarism often costs writers their careers and their respect. It can also harm the organizations who endorsed the writers.

Citing Sources

Creating plagiarism-free work is easier if you know why, when, and how to cite sources.

Why Cite Sources

The primary reason you always need to cite your sources is to avoid plagiarism. You should also cite your sources to:

- Tell your reader which ideas are not your own

  To omit a citation is to be dishonest to your readers because it misleads them to believe that you are responsible for others' ideas.

- Save time

  Citing a source properly can save you time if you need to refer back to the research. It can also save your readers time; if they need to refer to the source you referenced, the citation points them to the exact location of relevant content.

- Enhance the credibility of your work

  You can use citations to show your audience that your facts came from credible sources (such as peer-reviewed journals and well-known publications).

- Protect your academic and professional career from plagiarism's negative consequences

  The penalties of literary and intellectual theft in today's society can be severe. As you will see in the in the examples below, plagiarism not only hurts you as the writer, but also any person or organization that you represent.

University of Virginia   In 2001, 158 students attending the University of Virginia were accused of plagiarism. The accusations resulted in 20 expulsions, 28 voluntary drop outs, 90 exonerations, and multiple other "treatments" like counseling.[1]

Kaavya Viswanathan   In April 2006, this Harvard undergraduate student was accused of copying from up to three authors, and forty passages, in her novel *How Opal Mehta Got Kissed, Got Wild and Got a Life*.[2] As a result, the book publisher had to remove the unsold copies from the 100,000 first copies that had already been distributed to stores. Kaavya lost her two-book and movie deal and also cost Alloy Entertainment, who shared the book's copyrights.[3]

- Present your research ethically

  Even though intellectual "property" is intangible, taking it without asking is still comparable to stealing.

More Plagiarism Lessons from Real Life

Jayson Blair   In 2003, chaos erupted at the *New York Times* when the twenty-seven year old reporter was forced to resign after the newspaper found "fraud, plagiarism, and inaccuracies in 36 of his 73 articles."[4] Blair became the focus of a media-frenzy that negatively impacted the reputation of the *New York Times* as a credible news source.[5]

Lesson: If you plagiarize, you lose your audience's trust and gain nothing (besides negative attention).

Tom Squitieri   A sixteen-year veteran for *USA Today*, Tom Squitieri was forced to resign in May 2005 after it was revealed that he used quotations derived from other newspapers' articles without proper attribution in his own articles.[6]

Lesson: You can gain others' trust over years of ethical service, but once you break that trust by deceiving others through improper citation, you can lose your respect and your job very quickly.

Joe Biden   The Delaware senator, Joe Biden, lost his chance in the 1988 United States presidential campaign because he plagiarized part of a campaign speech.[7]

Lesson: Do not expect popularity, charisma, supporters, and money to save you from the consequences of plagiarism.

When to Cite Sources

Cite sources immediately where they are required. If you wait until you are finished writing your paper to go back and cite your sources, you may eventually become confused about which points even need citations. By delaying the citation process, you are more likely to direct your audience to the wrong source or forget to include some necessary citations altogether.

Cite all information or data that is not your own insight and is not common knowledge. Be careful not to mistake obscure information learned or memorized during research for common knowledge. To determine if information is common knowledge, see if it fits the criteria below.

Common Knowledge Is...

- Usually known before research or accepted as fact by most experts[8]

- Easily and quickly verifiable

- Something that your audience is already familiar with

- Typically included in introductory material on the subject[9]

Examples

capital cities, simple mathematics, notable dates in history, primary colors, water's chemical composition, major political figures' names and roles, planets' names

If you are still not sure if particular information or data you find during research is common knowledge, then be cautious and cite the source.

How to Cite Sources

Citing sources properly means following writing style rules. Writing styles are official methods that writers in common research fields follow to cite sources and format work in a consistent manner. Chapters 4-7 present the four major writing styles. Which writing style you should follow depends on which subject you are researching. Here are some general guidelines to help you determine which style to use and where to find it in this book.

- English or literature

  Refer to chapter 4 about the Modern Language Association rules

- Social sciences

  See chapter 5 for the American Psychological Association when researching communications, economics, education, anthropology, psychology, sociology or other soft sciences

- History

  See chapter 6 on the Chicago Manual of Style/Turabian

- Science

  Reference chapter 7 for the Council of Science Editors

Regardless of which writing style you use, be meticulous and conscientious about citing sources.

Using Copyrighted Works

A copyright, as stated by the U.S. Copyright office, gives an author or license holder the exclusive right to distribute, show, and prepare "derivative works" about the work, among other things. Consumers need the copyright holder's permission to copy a copyrighted work, unless their action and purpose constitutes fair use. When determining whether a copyright was infringed, courts use the four criteria set forth in section 107 of The Copyright Act of 1976.[10]

1. Purpose and character in using the work

   A nonprofit educational use is more likely to be a fair use than a commercial or entertainment use.[11]

2. Nature of the copyrighted work

   Fair use often involves non-fiction copyrighted work.

3. Amount and substantiality of the portion used in relation to the copyrighted work as a whole

   The greater the quantity of a copyrighted work you use, the higher the probability that you need permission to use to the copyrighted work.

4. Effect of the use upon the potential market or value of copyrighted work

   You probably need the copyright holder's permission if you use his or her work multiple times or distribute it to a "large public audience".[12]

Courts have recognized some general categories as fair use (criticism, comment, news reporting, teaching, scholarship, research and parodies)[13], but verifying fair use can still be confusing and controversial.

Notes

[1] Matthew Bowers, "Technology sniffing out a campus affliction: plagiarism," Daily Progress 17 Mar. 2007: N. pag. Media General. (27 Mar. 2007) <http://www.dailyprogress.com/servlet/Satellite?pagename=CDP/MGArticle/RTD_BasicArticle&c=MGArticle&cid=1173350262402>.

[2] News Hour Extra, 3 May 2006, MacNeil-Lehrer Productions, n.d., <http://www.pbs.org/newshour/extra/features/jan-june06/author_5-03.html>.

[3] David Mehegan, "Viswanathan book deal raises more questions," Boston Globe 29 Apr. 2006: N. pag. Boston.com. (27 Mar. 2007) <http://www.boston.com/news/globe/living/articles/2006/04/29/viswanathan_book_deal_raises_more_questions/>.

[4] Malcom Jones, "Have You Read This Story Somewhere?," Newsweek 139.4 (2 Apr. 2002): 10. EBSCOHost, 1 Apr. 2006 <http://search.epnet.com/>.

[5] "Top New York Times editors quit," CNN.com, 1 Mar. 2004, CNN, 19 May 2005 <http://www.cnn.com/2003/US/Northeast/06/05/nytimes.resigns/index.html>.

[6] Howard Kurtz, "USA Today Reporter Resigns," Washington Post 6 May 2005: C01. (19 May 2005) <http://www.washingtonpost.com/wpdyn/content/article/2005/05/05/AR2005050501876.html>.

[7] "In Brief," Quill 94.1 (Jan. 2006): 16-17. Communication & Mass Media Complete, EBSCO, Solomon Baker Library, Waltham, Ma, 7 Jan. 2007 <http://search.ebscohost.com/login.aspx?direct=true&db=ufh&AN=19750912&site=ehost-liveFootnote>.

[8] Incorporating References, 12 Mar. 2001, Johnson County Community College, 27 Mar. 2007 <http://staff.jccc.net/pmcqueen/Tips/references.htm>.

[9] Incorporating References.

[10] Copyright Law of the United States of America, 2007, U.S. Copyright Office, 30 Mar. 2007 <http://www.copyright.gov/title17/92chap1.html#107>.

[11] Copyright Fair Use Chart, 2007, University of Massachusetts Amherst, 30 Mar. 2007 <http://www.umass.edu/langctr/fu.html>.

[12] Copyright Fair Use Chart.

[13] Electronic Frontier Foundation, 21 Mar. 2002, 30 Mar. 2007 <http://www.eff.org/IP/eff_fair_use_faq.php>.

2   Research

This chapter contains fundamental information and tips that will guide you through each stage of the research process (selecting your topic, finding research materials from the library and the Internet, evaluating research materials, and tracking sources).

Choosing Your Topic

Although it is often overshadowed by the strenuousness of actually writing and researching a paper, choosing a strong topic is one of the most crucial steps in developing a solid paper. Here are some tips to help you select a good topic.

- Read over the assignment again.

    Highlight or circle your instructor's preferred writing style, page layout, and other important details including length requirements. Reading over the assignment several times during the writing and researching process will keep you focused on the task at hand.

- Make sure you understand the question completely.

    You have to know exactly what question you are facing before you can adequately attempt to answer it.

- Read your notes.

    Since many high school and college level papers require you to develop or expand on an idea or topic from class, looking over class material is a useful way to start the brainstorming process. If this does not help you to jumpstart your topic search, try other brainstorming methods. Draw an idea web, reflect on your personal interests, or peruse the library.

- Choose a topic that interests you!

    An engaging topic is the best gift that you can give yourself as a researcher. Pick something that piques your interest, something you want to know more about. Reading and writing about something that you are genuinely interested in makes researching seem a lot less like work.

- **Choose a topic that is feasible.**

  If your teacher specifies that the paper should be somewhere between five and seven pages, do not attempt to recount the entire history of imperial China. Make sure that your topic is not too elaborate or too obscure. With topics that are too elaborate, you run the risk of not finding a salient point for a thesis statement; with topics that are too obscure, you might not find sufficient research to bolster your argument.

- **Ask for help and suggestions from teachers and experts.**

  Talking to a teacher or an expert in your research area can add dimension, depth, and direction to your topic idea.

Developing a Working Thesis Statement

Once you select a general topic, you need to narrow your focus to researching a particular aspect of that topic. After that, you will need to narrow your focus even further to define your paper's purpose in a working thesis statement. To do this, you will need to know how to gather and work with preliminary sources.

Gathering Preliminary Sources

How you gather preliminary research materials depends on your familiarity with your chosen topic.

Situation A: You are not already familiar with your chosen topic.

Gather sources with general information about your topic. Look for texts that outline all of the major subtopics without overwhelming you with details. You can then choose which subtopics you would like to learn more about.

Situation B: You already understand your topic and have chosen one of its subtopics to research.

As you gather sources, verify that your preliminary research materials provide ample information about your chosen subtopic before you print or borrow them from the library.

Working with Preliminary Sources

Take notes as you read.

Write down any questions that arise for you as you learn about your topic. Also document your insights, confusions, and any contradictions or trends that you notice.

Identify each interesting topic discussion point.

After you compiled a list of interesting discussion points that other scholars have used in their work, decide which ones are most engaging to you. Your research paper will be an opportunity to analyze and react to other scholars' discussions.

Use your notes and list of discussion points to develop a working thesis statement.

Your notes should be full of your own ideas and reactions to what you have learned during your preliminary research. Therefore, they are a great place to look when you are ready to draft a working thesis statement, the first draft of the claim that you will make in your paper.

Check availability of sources that will contribute information to your paper.

Depending on how much information you find about your chosen topic, you may have to expand or narrow its breadth a few times before you finalize your thesis statement.

Expanding your Topic

If you initially are interested in writing about the psycho-social development of twelve-year-old boys, you might have to broaden your focus to the psycho-social development of all adolescent boys in order to gather enough information.

Narrowing your Topic

In another paper, you might initially choose to research the Stone Age. As you learn more about the Stone Age you can narrow your topic to cover a particular subject or idea, such as the study of stone tools. You can narrow your focus even further to stone tools in the Paleolithic Era and, if needed, you can further narrow your discussion to tools used during the upper, middle, or lower Paleolithic periods.

Think of your working thesis statement as a hypothesis that you will attempt to test through your research.

Keep in mind that you can use your paper to present your claim as being partially valid, if that is what you discover during research. Be honest about what your research reveals.

To learn how to write a thesis statement, see *Thesis Statements* on page 23.

Gathering Sources: Using the Library

You should go into the library with a relatively concrete idea of what you would like to write about (a working thesis statement) so that you can start your research immediately.

Finding Your Sources

By using the library's alphabetized card catalogue, you can look up sources by subject, author, or book title. With the advances in computer technology, card catalogues are becoming increasingly obsolete and consequently replaced by library databases. These computer catalogues facilitate the same searches with greater ease and efficiency. After entering the requested data into a library database, the computer will direct you to the places in the library where material that is relevant to your search is located.

Primary Versus Secondary Sources

When looking for information about your topic, keep the difference between primary and secondary sources in mind. Primary sources are firsthand, original, unedited works. These can be novels, diaries, pieces of artwork, letters, short stories, speeches, photographs, plays, poems, films, autobiographies, posters, etc. Secondary sources are sources that critique, comment, interpret, or analyze primary sources. Secondary sources are often books, critical essays, encyclopedias, reviews, dictionaries, and journal articles. Newspaper and magazine articles can be primary or secondary sources, depending on their subject matter. Instructors often require students to incorporate both primary and secondary sources into research papers.

Example

Jane Austen's *Pride and Prejudice* is a primary source. A critical essay about the writing techniques displayed in *Pride and Prejudice* is a secondary source.

Michelangelo's painting on the ceiling of the Sistine Chapel is a primary source. A critique of the ceiling in the Sistine Chapel is a secondary source.

An American slave narrative, like the *Narrative of Frederick Douglass, An American Slave*, is a primary source. An encyclopedia blurb about the narrative is a secondary source.

Knowing Your Resources

Most people know that you can access books, encyclopedias, almanacs, academic journals, magazines, newspapers, and videos in the library. People often overlook, or are unaware of, the less visible research venues of microfilm, microfiche, electronic databases, and interlibrary loans.

Some libraries possess microfilm and microfiche capabilities, where printed materials (typically old newspapers and magazines) are photographed and preserved in rolls of film to save library space. When looking through these rolls of film using the enlarger/projection machine that the library provides, you can find fascinating articles from various time periods that lend an interesting historical perspective to your research. The rolls of film are typically catalogued and indexed for user convenience.

As a student researcher, it is important to see if your school subscribes to electronic databases specifically geared at making the research process easier for students by providing full-text general, journal, and critical articles. *Academic Search Premier, Lexis Nexis, Encyclopedia Britannica Online,* and the *Oxford English Dictionary* are just a few examples of electronic databases that institutions and libraries provide for their students free of cost.

If you cannot find your desired book or source from a particular library, most libraries offer interlibrary loans, a system that enables your library to import books and other materials from surrounding libraries. Talk to your librarian and he or she will assist you in filling out the necessary request forms for an interlibrary loan.

Internet Research

You can gather research materials online more efficiently by selecting the right Web navigation tools. The tips in this section show you how to use the Internet to your advantage in each step of your research.

1. Select a research topic.

    Online directories, like the Open Directory Project (dmoz.org), divide web resources into categories. They generally list higher quality resources than search engines do because directories use people, instead of software, to evaluate the best Web sites and place them into the directories' appropriate categories. It can be more helpful to see a list of potential topics in a directory than to sort through thousands of search engine results.

2. Narrow your research focus.

If your research topic is broad, then it is likely to appear as a category within an online directory. You can choose a specific aspect of your topic to focus on by browsing its subcategories. To find more defined and credible subtopic resources, locate a directory that is entirely devoted to your topic.

3. Use respected sources.

You will want to be certain that field experts or scholars authored your sources. Visit your school or library's Internet databases to search for credible information related to your thesis. If you need help selecting or finding an appropriate database, then ask a librarian for advice.

4. Locate a specific fact or webpage.

The best method of locating a specific fact or Web page online is doing a search query using the unique (but pertinent) parts of the fact or page as keywords. If you tend to use a particular search engine, such as www.google.com, take the time to learn how to best execute an internet search. A Boolean search recognizes the commands AND, OR, and NOT in a search query, and narrows or expands the search engine's results accordingly.

For example, if you are looking for information about former President Clinton and Al Gore, you enter "President Clinton AND Al Gore" into the search box. All sites where both names are present will appear in the search results.

5. Find needed information.

You can find the information or facts you need by submitting your questions to a newsgroup or e-mail discussion group. You could refer to www.tile.net/news, a newsgroup directory, for help choosing appropriate newsgroups for your research topic.

6. Find current and relevant information.

Online newspaper publications, such as www.nytimes.com, provide current and well-dated information. Online broadcast news sites, like www.cnn.com, also provide an archive of searchable and well-dated information. Watching and listening to the multimedia on news sites is an excellent way to learn recent news about your topic that might not be available in books or on video yet.

Knowing how to gather information will help you save time to reflect on your research materials. By researching more efficiently, you give yourself more time to analyze, contemplate, and respond to sources in your notes, drafts, and the final research paper.

Evaluating Sources

Why should I evaluate my sources?

The quality of your paper is partially determined by the quality of your research sources. Pick and choose your sources wisely and understand the difference between a source that is credible and one that is not.

How do I evaluate my sources?

Use the credibility checklist and information on the following pages to ensure that you have chosen appropriate research materials.

Source Credibility Checklist

___ My research materials provide me with the most current information available.

With reference manuals, books, and articles, check the publication date to make sure that you have the most current version available. This is especially important with science and technology sources, as the accepted scholarship is prone to change very quickly.

___ There is evidence that Web sites' authors and owners have specialized knowledge of my research topic.

To find evidence of the author's expertise in a book, refer to the "About the Author" page. On a Web site, refer to the "About Us" page. In your article sources, read blurbs about the author's credentials and contact the organization if you are at all unsure of an author's credibility. The bibliography is also an excellent way to at least verify that the author uses accurate information from respectable sources.

___ My Web site sources have credible motives.

Non-profit organizations, denoted by .org in the Web address, are typically more reliable research sources than .biz or .com. Do your research on Web sites that have minimal to no advertisements and pop-ups. For the most part, the motive of the Web sites from which you gather information should be clearly educational--not profit based.

___ My research materials present information fairly.

When researching, you may come across authors and articles who articulate opposing viewpoints. In your writing, it is important that you recognize both sides of an argument. If you refer to a biased source, then try to balance its influence on your research conclusions by giving equal consideration to sources with opposing arguments. Be sure to show the reader that you consider all viewpoints.

Fig. 2.1. Source credibility checklist.

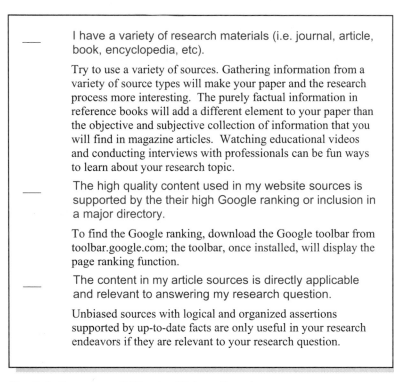

_____ I have a variety of research materials (i.e. journal, article, book, encyclopedia, etc).

Try to use a variety of sources. Gathering information from a variety of source types will make your paper and the research process more interesting. The purely factual information in reference books will add a different element to your paper than the objective and subjective collection of information that you will find in magazine articles. Watching educational videos and conducting interviews with professionals can be fun ways to learn about your research topic.

_____ The high quality content used in my website sources is supported by the their high Google ranking or inclusion in a major directory.

To find the Google ranking, download the Google toolbar from toolbar.google.com; the toolbar, once installed, will display the page ranking function.

_____ The content in my article sources is directly applicable and relevant to answering my research question.

Unbiased sources with logical and organized assertions supported by up-to-date facts are only useful in your research endeavors if they are relevant to your research question.

Fig. 2.1. Source credibility checklist continued.

Tracking Sources

Why should I track sources during research?

Organizational methods help you to keep track of your sources and record the information necessary to create an accurate bibliography. They can also help you find an effective way to plan your paper and organize ideas.

How do I organize my source information during research?

Using organization techniques, such as working SourceAid bibliographies, color coded notes, and the notecard method will help you stay focused and organized as you research and write.

Working SourceAid Bibliography

Method

As soon as you have your research materials, log in to SourceAid.com and enter your source information to create a revisable citation list. You can edit your citations later on if you save the citations as an online citation project or e-mail them to yourself. You do not need a finalized set of sources to start working on your citations; you can always delete citations if you do not end up using the source.

Color coded notes

Method

Gather an array of colored pens and your research materials. Use different pen colors as you take notes for different sources. When taking notes on your computer, you can use this same technique by changing font colors and styles for each source.

Notecard method

Method

Use notecards to record all quotations and citable material from your sources. Put one major thought or quotation on each notecard. On the back of these cards, place the information that you will need to build an accurate bibliography—author, book title, publisher, etc.

What information should I record?

The safest way to find the information that you will need for your citations is to refer to the *Citation Formats* section for your chosen writing style in this book. You can also log on to www.SourceAid.com to view source citation previews within the citation builder. See *Figure 2.2* and *Figure 2.3*.

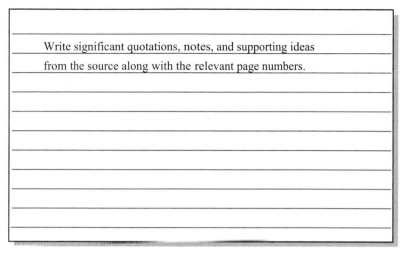

Fig. 2.2. The front of a notecard to cite a book.

Author -
Book title -
Editor -
Publication city -
Publisher -
Year published -

Fig. 2.3. The back of a notecard to cite a book.

3 Writing

A good research paper is an organized argument directed at supporting a thesis claim with the help of outside sources. This chapter explains how to write and structure an academic paper in chronological order, from organizing your ideas to making your final revisions. Though your paper writing process may not always be as linear as the following steps are arranged and explained, these steps nonetheless exemplify the key elements of a standard academic paper.

Paper Introductions

Introductory Paragraphs

The tone of your introductory paragraph should be focused and confident in order to convince the reader that the rest of the paper is worth reading. You can create an engaging and effective opening paragraph by drawing the reader into the paper with a strong leading sentence or pertinent quotation. Once you have captured the reader's attention with a solid first sentence, you need to start working toward the introduction of your thesis statement, your paper's main claim, which is usually best positioned at the end of your first paragraph. You can introduce your thesis by discussing the relevance of its topic with a few general sentences. As the paragraph progresses, make these sentences increasingly specific, so that the reader is eased into your thesis statement, the most precise sentence of your introduction.

Thesis Statements

What is a thesis statement?

One of the most important elements of any research paper is its thesis statement. The thesis statement is a brief explanation of your main claim or argument; it is usually a single sentence that summarizes the answer you give to the issue or question the paper addresses. The entire paper is an attempt to support the thesis statement.

Where is it located within my paper?

A thesis statement is typically located at the end of the paper's first paragraph.

When do I craft my thesis statement?

You need to construct your thesis statement after doing some research, when you are aware of the way you want to develop your paper and how you will arrange your argument.

To learn how to develop a working thesis statement, see *Developing a Working Thesis Statement* on page 10.

Body of the Paper

Topic Sentences

What is a topic sentence?

A topic sentence is the first sentence of a body paragraph that summarizes the paragraph's purpose in supporting the paper's thesis. The rest of the paragraph should support and prove its topic sentence. Use topic sentences to guide your reader through your argument with direction.

Starting with the first paragraph after the introduction, begin each paragraph with a topic sentence. A topic sentence resembles a thesis statement, but on a smaller scale. The thesis statement expresses your paper's main claim; a topic sentence is meant to be the "thesis statement" of each body paragraph.

How do I choose my topic sentences?

In outlining your paper and deciding how to prove your claim, work toward a resolution in steps. Each "step" is a new paragraph, summarized by a new topic sentence.

Organizing Your Ideas

Once you have completed your research and taken careful notes on the material that best supports your thesis claim, you might feel ready to start writing. Although your ideas are fresh in your mind and it is tempting to dive right into the writing process, you should slow down, collect your thoughts, and spend some time organizing your ideas on paper.

The most important element of organizing your ideas is mapping the progression of your argument, how you will prove your thesis statement in a logical order throughout the body of the paper. Here are three ways to organize your ideas for a research paper:

- Arranging your notecards

  If you followed the notecard method outlined on page 20, then you have supporting points for your thesis already written on notecards. Group the notecards according to the section of your thesis that they support. Determine the best way to arrange your argument to arrive at the conclusion or confirmation of your thesis claim. Rearrange your notecards again with the argument's order in mind. Your research is now arranged progressively.

- Cluster method/web diagramming

  After researching, you may feel like your ideas are jumbled and floating around haphazardly in your head. To combat this, sit down with a blank piece of paper and draw a cluster diagram of your thoughts. Put your main idea, your thesis, in the center of the page, and write all of the other ideas you want to mention in your paper around it. With all of your main ideas on paper, you can decide how you want to organize them. You can indicate groupings of ideas by drawing lines to connect them, See *Figure 3.1* for an example.

  Note: Cluster diagrams are also useful when brainstorming, determining a thesis, and selecting ideas you want to develop.

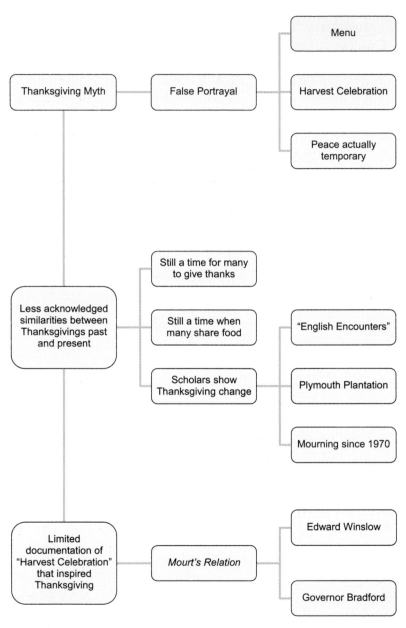

Fig. 3.1. Cluster diagram in development.

- Informal outlining

  Informal outlines can offer more flexibility in how you portray the progression of your argument. In its most basic form, an informal outline should present, in some way that makes sense to you, the components of the argument arranged in order. Just having a sketch, however brief, of the structure of the argument helps to keep you on track throughout the writing process. The skeleton of an informal outline can look something like this:

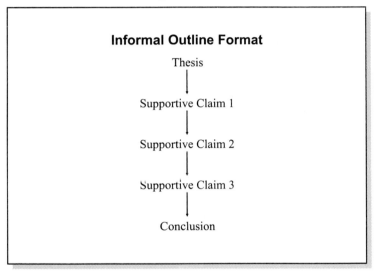

Fig. 3.2. Informal outline format.

Formal Outlines

When trying to organize your ideas, you may find it helpful to create a formal outline, one that follows the traditional Roman numeral format style. These outlines can look daunting from a distance, with many numbers and capitalized and un-capitalized letters, but they are just a more systematic way of presenting your ideas.

Formal Outline Format

Thesis Statement Sentence(s).

I.   First major point that supports the thesis.

     A. Point that supports the major point described in I.

         1. Aspect of point A.

         2. Aspect of point A.

     B. Point that supports the major point described in I.

         1. Aspect of point B.

         2. Aspect of point B.

II. Second major point that supports the thesis.

     A. Point that supports the major point described in II.

         1. Aspect of point A.

         2. Aspect of point A.

            a. Aspect of point made in II A 2.

            b. Aspect of point made in II A 2.

     B. Point that supports the major point described in II.

         1. Aspect of point B.

         2. Aspect of point B.

Fig. 3.3. Formal outline format.

Formal outlines require you to identify how your ideas are related in order to categorize them within the outline. What are your major points? What points support your major points? What points are tertiary? When you assign Roman numerals to each major point you need to make in proving your thesis, you also build topic sentences for your paper's body paragraphs. Supporting evidence, the capitalized A, B, Cs and 1, 2, 3s of each Roman numeral section, is the subject matter you will use to fill in each body paragraph, and prove each topic sentence (I, II, III). Each section needs at least two points; you cannot have just one sub-point or just one sub-topic.

There are three major types of outlines within this formal style:

- Topic outlines present the information within the outline topically without verb clauses or complete sentences. When working on a topic outline, it is important to uphold parallelism (agreement of verb noun, adjective, and verb forms).

- Sentence outlines, as their name implies, present each entry in sentence form using proper punctuation.

- Paragraph outlines, typically used for longer research papers, present each entry as a full paragraph with proper punctuation.

Sitting Down and Writing a Draft

What is a draft?

A draft is the first version of your paper. It is helpful to have a rough sketch of your organized and supported ideas so that you can work and rework these ideas to perfection.

Why should I draft?

Drafting helps you to solidify your outline, see if there is a flow to your ideas, and verify that your selected source quotations fit logically into your discussion. It allows you to write without apprehension or nervousness because the draft is not the final product. Drafts also help you see which subtopics in your paper need more supporting information in case you need to do more research.

When should I draft?

Begin drafting once you have a solid idea of what your thesis will be and how you can prove it. This should occur after you have organized your thoughts in an outline. By starting your draft on time, you can return to the library or your sources to find more specific information that you either did not find or deem relevant for your thesis in your initial search.

How do I draft?

Sit down with a clear idea of what you want to say and how you want to say it, and give yourself a reasonable time limit for drafting. Do not waste time and energy perfecting each sentence. Just write your ideas out as clearly as you can. Try to finish in the time that you allot for yourself and be prepared to make major revisions.

Incorporating Sources

What is a paraphrase?

A paraphrase is an indirect quotation, a translation of a quotation or idea from your sources into your own words. You do not need to put quotation marks around the paraphrased material, but you must remember to cite the original source at the end of the paraphrase—failing to do so is plagiarism.

When should I paraphrase?

Paraphrasing is helpful if you need to summarize information or when you want to communicate ideas in your own words. You can use paraphrases when your source's original wording is overly complex or obtuse.

Why paraphrase?

Being able to interpret the ideas articulated in your sources and communicate them in your own words lets your writing style shine through, exhibits your understanding of sources, and helps to keep a consistent flow to your paper.

How should I paraphrase?

It is impossible to paraphrase adequately without first understanding the meaning of the original source. Read over your source carefully and be sure to have a good grasp of the author's intended message before trying to summarize it in your own words.

You are writing a paper on Marx's notion of religion being the "opium of the people" and your original source includes the statement below:

"We do not know how much Marx understood about opium use in his day, but he certainly knew that it was a hallucinogenic and narcotic substance; it eased pain even as it created fantasies. And that, for him, is precisely the role of religion in the life of the poor."[1]

If you were to insert the original source into the paper, you would need to cite it properly and include the whole of the quotation in quotation marks.

Here is a possible paraphrase:

Marx understands the implications of saying that religion is the "opium of the people." He understands that the function of religion is something that eases pain and creates fantasies.

As a paraphrase, if you were to enter this into the body of your paper, you would not need to set it apart from the rest of your text with quotation marks, but you would need to cite the original publication at the end of your paraphrase.

Inserting Quotations

Incorporating direct quotations into your paper is another way of using your research findings to support your claim. Using quotations at key points in your paper can really bolster your argument and add validity to your thesis claim. Though using quotations can be quite helpful in articulating your point, be cautious not to overuse them—a paper replete with quotations can be a turn-off to your reader. Regardless of how well you have researched and how many good sources you have found to reference, quotations should serve only to endorse *your* ideas and thesis claim.

---

[1] Daniel L. Pals, Seven Theories of Religion (New York: Oxford University Press, 1996) n. pag.

When inserting quotations, be sure to put them in a context and explain their significance to your thesis. You cannot assume that the reader understands why you find a particular quotation relevant. You can present quotations clearly by using a signal phrase, one that connects the explanatory sentence and the quotation.

Example

In a recent interview, Ron Silvia described the importance of using SourceAid to create proper citations and preserve the academic integrity of the researcher. He discussed the plight of the plagiarizer. "Plagiarizers are subject to loss of respect and credibility."

Three Major Types of Quotations

The three major types of quotations are partial quotations, complete quotations, and block quotations

- Partial quotations

  Partial quotations include only the most applicable part of a sentence, be it a word or a phrase, in support of your thesis. Because it is not necessary to capitalize the first letter of the first word in a quotation when you are not quoting a full sentence, these types of quotations can be incorporated into your sentences discreetly, but they still require proper citations.

Example

According to Ron Silvia, students lose more than a valuable academic experience when they plagiarize; they also suffer a "loss of respect and credibility."

- Complete quotations

  Incorporate complete quotations into your composition if they are substantive and your content benefits from including the whole sentence(s).

- Block quotations

  When your quotation is three or more typed lines long, set it apart from the rest of the text using a block quotation. Single-space a block quotation and indent 1 inch from the left margin. Block quotations do not require quotation marks. They are particularly helpful when you want to analyze the section that you are quoting so the reader has the original text as a reference when reading your claim. This quotation format is typically used in citing poetry.

Example

In "The Love Song of J. Alfred Prufrock", T. S. Eliot is asking lofty questions about what it means to be human. In lines 45-48, the narrator is questioning his own potential and self-validity in a world that is inconstant:

Do I dare

Disturb the universe?

In a minute there is time

For decisions and revisions which a minute will reverse.

Tables and Figures

Including tables or figures in your paper can be a good way of presenting necessary information in a manner that is visually engaging and accessible to the reader. Tables and figures allow you to convey ideas and information clearly without relying exhaustively on explanatory sentences. Tables are particularly useful in representing data-intensive information.

Each writing style has its own rules about the proper placement and format of tables and figures; these guidelines are summarized in the later chapters that deal with each writing style individually. Please refer to the appropriate writing style chapter and table/figure guidelines before incorporating tables or figures into your text.

Paper Conclusions

Concluding Paragraph

The conclusion is...

The conclusion is the last paragraph of your paper and the place to express your closing thoughts. The conclusion also reiterates your thesis and highlights insights from the body of the paper. Before writing the conclusion, read over your paper from start to finish and recall the paper's most significant points.

The good thing about the conclusion is...

If you have written a paper that is true to its thesis statement, the conclusion should be easy to write. The conclusion is often a fitting place to explain your own input about the subject matter and say what the researching experience has taught you. In some research papers, it may be appropriate to pose a problem that arose during writing or research that could be relevant for future research.

The conclusion is important because...

The conclusion contains the final words in your paper and it is, consequently, the last impression you may make on the reader. By this point, the reader has read all of the facts that you have presented to support your main assertion. Use the last paragraph to restate the conclusions that arose from your research truthfully. Write your conclusion with confidence in your research, thesis, and supportive claims.

Making Revisions

After finishing a draft of your paper, be it a rough draft or something more polished, it is always beneficial to read it over and revise it. Here are some revision tactics to help you improve your paper.

- Look for specific types of problems as you proofread and edit.

  Because it is easy to feel overwhelmed by problems in your paper, try to focus on specific problems each time you read through the paper. For example, if you easily confuse verb tenses or have trouble keeping a consistent voice in writing, target these mistakes in your initial revision. After correcting the particular writing or grammar problems that usually trouble you, the remaining problems will become easier to detect.

- Be your own harshest critic.

  Give yourself some time to relax after writing the paper before returning to it with a fresh mindset. Distancing yourself from your paper will help you to obtain the more objective perspective that you need for effective revisions. When you are ready, print out a hard copy of the paper and begin crossing things out, adding things in, and writing new ideas in the margins. Do not be afraid to break down your ideas so that you can rebuild them with stronger connections and more support. See the revision checklist on the next page to verify that you have successfully revised your paper.

Revision Checklist

____ I am positive that my spelling and grammar are correct, and that my verb tenses and tone are consistent throughout the entire paper.

____ I considered rearranging (or have actually rearranged) all of the following: the paragraphs, the sentences within the paragraphs, and the words within the sentences.

____ I have made sure that each sentence contributes to my main discussion point.

____ I removed excess content that does not relate to my assertions.

____ I checked to see which arguments needed more supporting facts and I have, in turn, strengthened those arguments.

____ I used the peer review method by asking my peers to answer the questions in the subsequent section of this book.

____ I responded to my peers' suggestions with further independent revisions.

____ I conducted the peer review session again after I made my peers' suggested revisions.

____ I sought help from my instructor when I needed it by asking him or her specific questions.

____ I used my school's writing center (if applicable).

Fig. 3.4. Revision checklist.

- Invite close friends and peers to be honest critics.
  Try the peer review method by imploring others' help and being open-minded to their advice. To see if others understand your paper exactly as you want them to, ask them these questions:

Questions for Peer Review

1. What is the paper's main objective? (i.e. to claim that..., to explain how..., to debate whether..., to contrast..., etc...)

2. What points support this objective?

3. What grammatical problems do you see in the paper?

4. What structural problems do you see in the paper?

5. What would make the paper more convincing?

6. Which parts of the paper are unclear, if any?

7. Do any components seem irrelevant? Explain.

8. What other comments do you have about my paper?

9. What are the strong points of the paper? What makes them strong?

Fig. 3.5. Questions for peer review.

4 Modern Language Association

About MLA

What is MLA?

The information and examples provided in this chapter are consistent with the writing style set forth in the *MLA Handbook for Writers of Research Papers*, 6th Edition, as published by the Modern Language Association of America. The Modern Language Association's writing style, MLA, is the leading means of documentation in literary disciplines.

When should I use MLA?

Use the MLA writing style when working in the English and literary disciplines.

How is MLA different?

The MLA style privileges author information, finding it more pertinent than information regarding the publication date.

Composition Layout

These guidelines will help you properly format your paper. See also *Figure 4.2* through *Figure 4.4* for further help with formatting your research paper.

Paper
Use standard paper size (8 ½ x 11 inches).

Font
Use 12 point Times New Roman for the text body, quotations, and notes.

Margin
Use a 1 inch margin around the text body.

Header text
Begin numbering pages in the upper-right corner of the header immediately following your last name.

Heading
Left-align the heading on the first full page of text 1 inch from the top of the page. The appropriate format is as follows:

Format
Name
Teacher or professor's name
Class name and Course number
Day Month Year

Title
Center-align the title (without italics, quotation marks, or an underline) one double-spaced line below the heading on the same page as the beginning of your text. Although title pages are not required by MLA guidelines, your teacher might still require you to attach a title page with his or her own formatting specifications.

Spacing

Double-space throughout the text body, any quotations (except block quotations), notes, and citations.

Alignment and indentation

Indent the first word of each paragraph by ½ inch. For block quotations, indent 1 inch.

Tables

Insert a table close to its relevant content in the text body. Give a title, such as `Table #`, followed by a title case description above the table. Cite the source as a note immediately below the table. If you need to include a content note with the table, use a letter in place of the note number and place the note below the source citation.

Table #

Write a Description Here.

	Insert table here.	

Source: Insert note citation here.

Letter Superscript Content note.

Fig. 4.1. Format to include a table in your research.

Figures

Include the label `Fig. #`, a description, and the citation directly below all charts, diagrams, or illustrations in your text.

Ch. 4

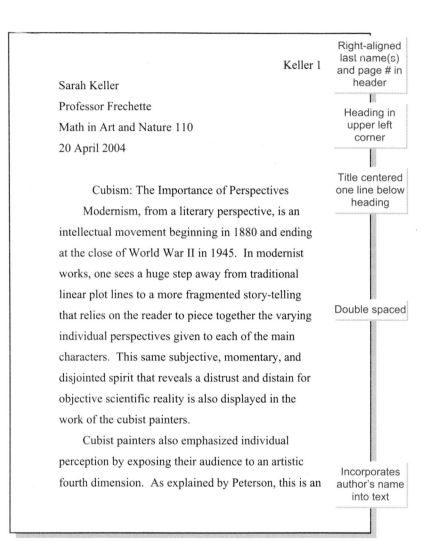

Keller 1

Right-aligned
last name(s)
and page # in
header

Sarah Keller

Professor Frechette

Math in Art and Nature 110

20 April 2004

Heading in
upper left
corner

Cubism: The Importance of Perspectives

Modernism, from a literary perspective, is an

intellectual movement beginning in 1880 and ending

at the close of World War II in 1945. In modernist

works, one sees a huge step away from traditional

linear plot lines to a more fragmented story-telling

that relies on the reader to piece together the varying

individual perspectives given to each of the main

characters. This same subjective, momentary, and

disjointed spirit that reveals a distrust and distain for

objective scientific reality is also displayed in the

work of the cubist painters.

Cubist painters also emphasized individual

perception by exposing their audience to an artistic

fourth dimension. As explained by Peterson, this is an

Title centered
one line below
heading

Double spaced

Incorporates
author's name
into text

Fig. 4.2. Body page layout.

Keller 2

added dimension consisting of time or spatial

relations, "an avenue of escape from conventional

representation" (36). As exemplified in both analytic

and synthetic cubism, cubist painters were

preoccupied with "new possibilities of spatial

measurement", namely with the idea of a fourth

dimension (Kaufman par. 4). The intention behind

this goal was to "grasp the ideal and the

transcendental and to encompass the infinite and

infinitesimal" (Peterson 36). Even though in this three

dimensional world, the fourth dimension necessarily

remains a concept and not a reality, the artistic quest

for portraying such a world proves the desire to view

the universe from a different perspective than the one

afforded us by our human minds. It highlights, yet on

Paragraph and page references direct reader to specific location of information in sources

Ch. 4

Fig. 4.3. Body page layout continued.

Keller 6

Works Cited

Bradbury, Malcolm, and James McFarlane. "The

Name and Nature of Modernism." *Modernism: A*

Guide to European Literature 1890-1930.

London: Penguin Group, 1991. 19-55.

Henderson, L. *The Fourth Dimension and Non-*

Euclidean Geometry in Modern Art. Princeton,

NJ: Princeton University Press, 1983. 44-116.

Kaufman, Jason. "Pioneering Cubism." *Jason*

Edward Kaufman. 2004. 8 April 2004.

<http://www.jasonkaufman.com/articles/

picasso_and_braque.htm >.

Peterson, Ivars. "A Place in Space." *Fragments of*

Infinity: A Kaleidoscope of Math and Art. New

York: John Wiley & Sons, 2001. 35-60.

Title without special font effects

Double spaced

First line in citation is left-aligned and subsequent lines are ½"

Document all sources cited in the paper

Fig. 4.4. Works Cited page layout.

Works Cited

A Works Cited page is a carefully organized list of the bibliographic information for each source that you have cited in your paper.

When should I begin creating a Works Cited page?

You should begin creating your Works Cited page as soon as you find the research materials that you plan to cite in your paper. If you are not sure whether you will use the ideas or words from one of your sources, it is best to include it in your working works-cited list. If you create your Works Cited page with the SourceAid citation builder, then you will be able to delete un-cited sources easily anytime during the research process.

Works Cited Page Layout

Contents
Include each source that you referenced in your paper.

Pagination
Insert the page number in the header ½ inch below the top of the page as a continuation from the text.

Title
Center the title, Works Cited, 1 inch below the top of the page.

Spacing
Double-space throughout the entire Works Cited page. Double-space the line between the title and the first entry. Also double-space the lines between and within all citations so that the space between every line is equal.

Alignment and indentation
Align the first line of each citation with the left margin. Indent subsequent lines ½ inch.

Ordering citations

Arrange citations in alphabetical order. If a citation begins with an article (The, A, or An), then use the next word in the citation to place it alphabetically in the works-cited list. See *Ordering Citations: Special Circumstances* for more details.

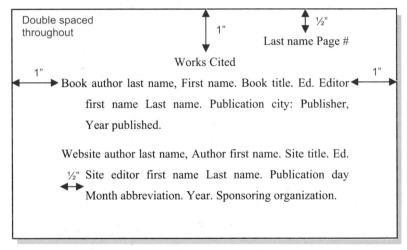

Double spaced throughout

1"

½"

Last name Page #

Works Cited

1" → Book author last name, First name. Book title. Ed. Editor ← 1"

first name Last name. Publication city: Publisher, Year published.

Website author last name, Author first name. Site title. Ed. ½" Site editor first name Last name. Publication day Month abbreviation. Year. Sponsoring organization.

Fig. 4.5. The beginning of a works-cited list.

Choosing the Right Kind of MLA Source List

If a traditional Works Cited page does not satisfy your research purposes adequately, then you might want to consider using another type of MLA source list. You may choose to include explanations, descriptions, or insight with your citations in an Annotated List of Works Cited, or you might opt to include information about sources that you did not cite in your paper in a List of Works Consulted.

Annotated List of Works Cited

The MLA annotated citation consists of the bibliographic citation followed with a short note. The note appears one double-spaced line below the citation.

Format

Bibliographic Information.

Annotation.

Works Consulted

If you include sources that you do not cite in your paper, then title your source list Works Consulted.

Selected List of Works Consulted

If you include sources that you do not cite in your paper but want to recommend to your readers, then title your source list Selected List of Works Consulted.

Ordering Citations: Special Circumstances

Citations in MLA works-cited lists are arranged in alphabetical order, but this can be difficult to do in particular situations.

Two names that begin with same letters

Alphabetize names by comparing them one letter at a time while disregarding punctuation and spaces in the names.

Suppose you have to alphabetize two sources. One is by Adam Marcus and another is by Samantha Marks.

In the works-cited list, the source written by Adam Marcus would come first because the first unique letter in his last name (the letter c) precedes the first unique letter in Marks (k).

Marcus, Samantha

Marks, Adam

Two authors with same last name

To order citations with identical last names compare the letters in the authors' first names.

> Suppose you are trying to arrange the citations for a source by Barbara Michaels and another source by Steven Q. Michaels. The citation for Barbara Michaels' book would precede the citation for Steven Q. Michaels' journal article because the first letter in her first name (B) comes before S, the first letter in Steven.
>
> Michaels, Barbara.
>
> Michaels, Steven Q.

Two sources by same author

When citing two sources by the same author, put them in alphabetical order by comparing the letters in the part of the citation that follows the author's name (usually the source title).

> Suppose you referenced two of Leo Tolstoy's books, *Anna Karenina* and *War and Peace*. The citation for *Anna Karenina* would precede the citation for *War and Peace* because the A (in Anna) comes before W (in War) in the alphabet.
>
> Tolstoy, Leo. Anna Karenina.
>
> Tolstoy, Leo. War and Peace.

Source where article is first word in title

When alphabetically arranging your works-cited list, exclude articles (The, A, An) from a source title if it is the first word in the title.

Example

"New England Nun" instead of "A New England Nun."

Unforgotten Heart: An anthology of short stories instead of The Unforgotten Heart: An anthology of short stories

Source by author with pen name

To cite the author's real name in addition to his or her pseudonym, cite the pseudonym first. Follow it with the real name in brackets, with no added punctuation between the pen name and the real name.

Format

Author pseudonym last name, First name [Author real first name Last name].

Example

Westmacott, Mary [Agatha Christie].

Source by author with title

Do not include titles in your citations. Omit title names such as PhD, Saint, President, and the like.

If the author has a title that is essential to his or her name (i.e. VII or Jr.), then include it using the format below:

Format

[Author last name], [First name] [Middle initial]. [Essential title]

Note: Do not forget to put a comma between the author's name and the essential title.

Parenthetical Citations

Purpose

You need to cite sources within your work to show the reader precisely which parts of your paper come from an outside source and identify the source of each borrowed word, concept, or fact. For more general information, see *Incorporating Sources* on page 30.

Function

In-text citations provide readers with enough information about a source (last name and page numbers) to direct them to the correct citation in the works-cited list, enabling them to see the publication information for the source being cited.

Components

In-text citations typically include the author's last name and the source's relevant page numbers without punctuation or abbreviations.

Format variations

The two basic ways of integrating a citation into your text are shown below.

You can cite the author's name in your text.

Format

Author last name Sentence (Page number(s)).

Example

Susan Corning's research paper about the past, present, and future status of the Environmental Protection Agency shows why protecting the environment is a "global issue" (71).

You can also cite the author's last name before the page number in the parentheses.

Format

Sentence (Author last name Page number starts-Ends).

Example

"The world population is not increasing exponentially" (Smith 99).

Parenthetical Citations: Special Circumstances

Sometimes citing the author's last name and the page number or location of cited material is not enough to help the reader find the corresponding citation on the Works Cited page. Use the guidelines in this section to determine if and how you should include more information in a parenthetical citation.

No author

Cite the first component of the works-cited list entry in your parenthetical citation.

Listed by editor or translator's name

If an entry in the list of works-cited begins with an editor or translator's name, then cite that last name at the start of the citation in place of the author's.

Listed by title

If the source is cited by its title in the works-cited list, then cite the title in your text along with the page or location from which the information was borrowed in the source.

Format

("Title," Page number)

Ch. 4

Multiple authors

Two or three authors

Cite each author's last name and the exact page numbers or location referenced in the source.

Format

(Author 1 and Author 2 Page number)

(Author 1, Author 2, Author 3 Page number)

Example

"Recent studies suggest that flu germs can survive on your toothbrush for up to one day" (Beverly, Norton, Fitz ch. 6).

Four or more authors

Cite the first author's last name followed by `et al.` and the exact page numbers or location referenced in the source.

Example

(Posh et al. 72-81).

Group author

Cite the group author's name along with the page number. If the author's name is long, including the name in the paper's text can help increase readability and flow of your paper. This type of in-text citation will prevent the reader from being distracted by a long parenthetical reference.

Example

In February 2003, yet another spokesperson at the Ida Simms Research Institute supported this when he pointed out that "one of the keys to productivity is to allow your brain to function properly by giving it the nutrients that it needs" (par. 3).

If you want to cite the author's name in the parentheses, then abbreviate parts of the name when appropriate.

Example

In February 2003, yet another spokesperson supported this when he pointed out that "one of the keys to productivity is to allow your brain to function properly by giving it the nutrients that it needs" (Ida Simms Research Inst. par. 3).

Two authors with identical last names

Cite the author's first initial with his or her last name.

Example

"Doctor Klyde recommends taking the pill twice daily with eight ounces of liquid" (M. Cleary 12).

Sources without pages

When a source does not have page numbers, use other types of location identifiers and their appropriate abbreviations when possible.

Text Division Type	Parenthetical Reference Format
Line	(Author last name line number) (Author last name line number starts-ends)
Chapter	(Author last name ch. number)
Paragraph	(Author last name par. number) (Author last name pars. number)
Section	(Author last name sec. number)

Multivolume works

To cite a particular piece of information from a volume when you have two or more volumes of a multivolume work cited in your works-cited list, cite the exact volume from which the information was borrowed followed by a colon, 1 space, and the page number.

Example

Veronica hints that she is frustrated with her progress when she says, "I don't want to try anymore! I have hit a plateau" (Daily 2: 203).

To cite an entire volume when you have two or more volumes of a multivolume work cited in your works-cited list, cite the volume as a whole without page numbers. When citing an entire volume in parentheses use the abbreviation `vol.`. Separate the abbreviation from the author's name with a comma.

Example

(Schmidt, vol. 6)

When citing an entire volume within the sentence, spell out the word `volume`.

Example

Schmidt duplicates the nature theme in volume 6 with her frequent but indirect references to roots, branches, blooming, growth, and cycles.

Two or more sources

Combine parenthetical citations in traditional format inside one set of parentheses by listing them one by one, using semicolons to separate each source. Avoid interrupting the reader with lengthy in-text citations by using notes.

Format

(Source 1; Source 2; Source 3)

Example

(Hunt 4; Bilton ch. 7; Parker par. 3)

Notes

Notes as a place to include extra information

Extra information that is relevant but not essential to your thesis can be included with your paper in footnotes or endnotes.

Content notes can be used for different reasons. They can briefly explain the reasoning behind your source selection or research method and provide supplementary detail that concisely illuminates a claim made in your paper.

Example

Footnoted sentence:

With a 10% margin of error, you can expect that 80 of the students in my tenth grade classes will do at least average quality homework.[18]

Footnote:

[18] Average quality is defined as earning 75% or better on each assignment and turning in all but one assignment on time.

Notes as documentation

As a substitute for parenthetical documentation, citations in footnotes and endnotes identify the source and the page numbers that contain information you have included in your text.

This use of notes for documentation requires you to insert superscripted numbers into your text next to any borrowed information. The numbers direct the reader to the corresponding citation either on a separate page or in the page's footer depending on whether the source's citations are in end or footnote form. In some cases, endnotes can take the place of a works-cited list.

Choosing between Endnotes and Footnotes

If you are going to use notes to document sources quoted directly or indirectly throughout your paper but are not sure whether footnotes or endnotes would be more appropriate, consider the points below when making your decision.

Ch. 4

Ch. 4

Preference

In most cases, it is best to use endnotes rather than footnotes when documenting sources referenced throughout your paper. Endnotes do not distract the reader from the text body because they are located on a separate page.

Format differences

Footnote and endnote citations are the same, with the exception of their location within the research paper and line spacing.

Endnotes

Location

Allocate the next blank page after the end of the text body as a place to put your endnotes.

Page title

Title the endnotes page `Notes` and center it 1 inch from the top of the page.

Pagination

Number the `Notes` page(s) as a continuation from the text.

Indentation

Indent the first line of each citation by ½ inch. Align subsequent lines with the left margin.

Number

Superscript the arabic number at the beginning of each citation and follow it with one space. The first endnote number should appear as [1] `citation.`, the second endnote number should appear as [2] `citation.`, and so on.

Spacing

Double-space throughout the page, both within and between endnote citations.

Footnotes

Location

Insert footnotes four lines below the body paragraph text in the footer of the page to which the footnote applies.

Spacing

Single-space within each footnote, but double-space between them.

Indentation

Indent the first line of each citation by ½ inch. Align subsequent lines with the left margin.

Number

Superscript the arabic number at the beginning of each citation and follow it with 1 space. The first endnote number should appear as [1] `citation.`, the second endnote number should appear as [2] `citation.`, and so on.

Continuing footnotes on the next page

To continue a footnote on the next page, begin by inserting a solid line one double-spaced line below the last line of text on the next page. Continue the footnote one double-spaced line below the solid line. The footnotes that apply to that next page continue below the carried over footnote.

First note references

The first time that you refer to a particular source in your paper with a foot or endnote, you need to provide a complete note citation called a first note reference. A first note reference includes all citation components that are necessary for the reader to independently find the same source and specific information that you referenced in your paper.

Format

Note [#] Author first name Middle initial. Last name, Book title (Publication city: Publisher name, Year published) Page number starts-Ends.

Ch. 4

Example

[2] Bill C. Ports, <u>Mr. Mechanic</u> (Peabody: Auto Club, 1978) 1-4.

Subsequent note references

After referring to a particular source once in a note citation, include only partial information in subsequent note references to the same source. These partial note references must give the reader enough information to find the source's publication information in the works-cited or first note reference. As shown in the sample format and example below, the author's last name followed by a space and the page number(s) is usually sufficient.

Format

Note # Author last name Page number starts-Ends.

Example

[5] Ports 8.

Notes: Special Circumstances

Sometimes including the author's last name and citing page numbers does not provide readers with enough information to identify which source is being referenced. A few special circumstances are explained below.

Two works by the same author

To help the reader identify which source you referenced, include the title of the work in subsequent note citations.

Format

Note # Author last name, Source title (shortened if long) Cited page number starts-Ends.

Example

² Smith, The Sand House 43-47.

Consecutive note references to one source

If you cite the same source two times in a row, then include a note citation for that source both times. Remember to include only partial note references to sources you have cited previously with a note.

Frequently Asked Questions

Browse the list of FAQ topics below to find the topic(s) relating to your question.

Question topics

A. Full versus partial note references
B. Formatting partial note references
C. Partial notes references with two sources by same author
D. The need for notes and works cited citations

A. **Do I need to include all of a source's information in a note citation if I cite the source repetitively throughout my paper?**

Full publication information only appears in the first note reference to a source. Subsequent notes include only partial citations because the remainder of the information is available in the works-cited list.

B. **If I have already cited a source in a note earlier in my paper, how do I cite it again in subsequent notes?**

Usually indicating the author's last name, along with the pagination, is enough to help your reader find the source's complete information in the list of works-cited or the source's first note.

Format

Note # Author last name, Page number starts-Ends.

Example

¹ Verne, 53.

While some authors use the abbreviations `ibid.`, `op.`, or `cit.` to point readers to the previous citation, it is better to simply repeat the information.

C. How do I cite a second (third, fourth, etc...) note reference for a source by the same author as another source?

If you have two or more sources by the same author, then include the title as well.

Format

Note # Author last name, <u>Source title</u> Page number starts-Ends.

Example

¹ Verne, <u>20,000 Leagues Under the Sea</u> 53.
² Verne, <u>Journey to the Center of the Earth</u> 29-30.

D. If I document my sources in note citations, do I still need a works-cited list?

If you use notes for your primary source documentation, you may not need to include a list of works cited. Check your assignment guidelines before choosing your citation method. See the next section to learn about the differences between notes and works-cited list citations.

Notes versus Works-Cited List Citations

This section compares and contrasts the content and format of notes and bibliographic citations to ensure that you do not plagiarize inadvertently by confusing their guidelines.

Table 4.1

Format and Content Comparison

Bibliographic Citations	Note Citations
Three sections	Four sections
1. Author last name, First name	1. Author first name Last name
2. Title	2. Title
3. Publication data not in parentheses	3. Parenthetical publication data
Page numbers of entire work	4. Page number(s) of information incorporated into text
Sections separated by periods	Sections separated by commas

Understanding MLA Terminology

MLA specifies how to cite publication dates and abbreviations. In most cases, to ensure clarity and formality, it is best not to abbreviate within the body of your paper.

Publication Dates

How you cite publication dates depends on the source type and frequency of publication.

Table 4.2

Date format by Source Type/Publication Frequency

Date format	Source type or publication frequency
Year	edition(s)
Year, Month	journals, books, audiovisual media, meetings, magazines, newsletters, and newspapers (include day if included on the publication)
Year, Month, Day	dailies and weeklies

Missing Citation Components

To indicate that citation information is unknown as opposed to incorrectly omitted, use the abbreviations in the table below.

Table 4.3

Abbreviations for Missing Information

Missing Component	Abbreviation
Date	n.d.
Publication information	n.p.
Page number(s)	n. pag.

Commonly Abbreviated Terms

Use the abbreviated form of the following commonly used terms for accurate and concise citations. Do not abbreviate these terms in the body of your paper.

Table 4.4

Common Abbreviations

Common Terms	Abbreviations	Common Terms	Abbreviations
Book	bk.	multi-user domain, object oriented	MOO
Column	Col.	narrated by	narr.
Compact disc read-only memory	CD-ROM	Number	no.
Congress	cong.	Opus	op.
Department	dept.	Paragraph	par.
Dictionary	Dict.	Performed by	perf.
Dissertation	Diss.	Produced by	prod.
editor, edition, edited by	ed.	Quoted	qtd.
Encyclopedia	encyc.	Report	rept.
Example	ex.	Saint	St.
Figure	Fig.	Section	Sec.
for example	e.g.	Stanza	st.
Government	govt.	that is	i.e.
illustrator, illustration, illustrated by	illus.	translator, translation, translated by	trans.
Institution	Inst.	Version	vers.
Introduction	introd.	video home system	VHS
Multi-user domain	MUD	written by	writ.

Ch. 4

Commonly abbreviated works-cited list terms

When creating your works-cited list, be sure to abbreviate the following units of time, dates, and locations.

Table 4.5

Works-Cited List Abbreviations

Works-Cited List Terms	Abbreviations
Time	Abbreviate time units.
Second	sec.
Minute	min.
Hour	hr.
Morning	a.m.
Afternoon and Night	p.m.
Date	Abbreviate dates.
Day	Abbreviate days of the week.
	Sun. Mon. Tues. Wed. Thurs. Fri. Sat.
Week	wk.
Month	Abbreviate all months (except for May, June, and July).
	Jan. Feb. Mar. Apr. May June July Aug. Sept. Oct. Nov. Dec.
Year	yr.
Century	Cent.
Location	Abbreviate state and country names.
State	State abbreviations should be in all caps and do not contain periods.
	CA NH NY VA MA CO
Country and Province	Abbreviate country names.
	US Jap. It. Austral. Isr. QC

Citation Formats

Before creating your MLA citations, make sure you have looked over the Use the note examples in this section to format first note references only. For help formatting subsequent note references see *Subsequent note references* on page 58.

If MLA has not specified a citation format for the source you are citing, use citation formats for similar source types as models to cite the source.

0.　Multiple Authors and Editors

The formats below show how to cite sources with multiple editors and authors. Before referring to the formats, you should be aware of these two general rules for citing sources with multiple authors:

1.　Number of Authors to Include

Cite no more than three authors in a citation. If there are four or more authors, cite *only the first* author's name followed by `, et al.`.

2.　Order of Authors in Citation

Do not automatically cite authors' names in alphabetical order within the citation. Instead, order authors' names in the same sequence as they appear on the source's title page.

0a.　Up to Three Authors

Works Cited Entry

Author 1 last name, First name Middle initial., Author 2 first name Middle initial. Last name, and Author 3 first name Middle initial. Last name.

Note

Author 1 first name Middle initial. Last name, Author 2 first name Middle initial. Last name, and Author 3 first name Middle initial. Last name.

0b.   Editor(s) with Author(s)

Cite the authors' names first, followed by the source title and the editor(s). Use the abbreviation Ed. in works cited entries to indicate editors' names in edited books with authors. Use the abbreviation ed. to do the same with notes.

The following format example shows how to cite a source with two authors and two editors.

Works Cited Entry

Author last name, First name Middle initial., and Author first name Middle initial. Last name. <u>Source title</u>. Ed. Editor first name Middle initial. Last name and Editor first name Middle initial. Last name.

Note

Author first name Middle initial. Last name, and Author first name Middle initial. Last name, <u>Source title</u>, ed. Editor first name Middle initial. Last name and Editor first name Middle initial. Last name.

0c.   Editor(s) (No Author)

To cite one editor without an author, put , ed. after the editor's name

Works Cited Entry

Editor last name, First name Middle initial., ed.

Note

Editor first name Middle initial. Last name., ed.

Ch. 4

0d. Translators

In a works cited entry, put the abbreviation Trans. after the source title and immediately before the translator's name.

Works Cited Entry

Author last name, First name Middle initial. <u>Source title</u>. Trans. Translator first name Middle initial Last name.

Example

```
Homer. Odyssey. Trans. W.H.D. Rouse. New York:
    New American Library, 1999.
```

If the translator is the same as the editor, use the format Trans. and ed. in a works cited citation.

Example

```
Lama, Dalai. How to Practice the Way to a
    Meaningful Life. Trans. and ed. Jeffrey
    Hopkins. New York: Pocket Books, 2002.
```

Note

In a note citation, put the abbreviation trans. after the source title and before the translator's name.

If the translator is the same as the editor, use the format trans. and ed. in a note citation.

Example

```
    ¹ Dalai Lama, How to Practice the Way to a
Meaningful Life, trans. and ed. Jeffrey
Hopkins (New York: Pocket Books, 2002) 45.
```

0e. Compilers

Works Cited Entry

To cite a translation with a compiler in a works cited entry, put a `Comp.` right before the compiler's name. If the compiler is also the editor, then use `Ed. and comp.` to the left of the editor/compiler's name in the works-cited list.

Author last name, First name Middle initial. <u>Source title</u>. Comp. Compiler first name Middle initial Last name.

Example

Carrol, Lewis. <u>Alice's Adventures in Wonderland</u>. Comp. Cooper Edens.

Note

To cite a compiler's name in a note entry, put a `comp.` after the source title and right before the compiler's name. If the translator is also the compiler, use the format `trans. and comp.`.

Example

[1] Lewis Carrol, <u>Alice's Adventures in Wonderland</u>, comp. Cooper Edens.

1. Advertisement

1a. Published

Works Cited Entry

Company or product advertised. Advertisement. <u>Publication title</u>. Date published day Month abbreviation Year: Page number starts-Ends.

Example

VISA. Advertisement. <u>People</u>. 18 July 2005: 70.

Note

[Note #] Company or product advertised, advertisement, <u>Publication title</u> Date published day Month abbreviation Year: Page number starts-Ends.

Example

¹ VISA, advertisement, <u>People</u> 18 July 2005: 70.

1b. Television

Works Cited Entry

Company or product advertised. Advertisement. Television network name. Date published day Month abbreviation Year.

Example

Volvo S60. Advertisement. National Broadcast Company. 13 June 2005.

Note

^(Note #) Company or product advertised, advertisement, Television network name Date published day Month abbreviation Year.

Example

¹ Volvo S60, advertisement, National Broadcast Company 25 July 2005.

1c. Online

Works Cited Entry

Company or product advertised. Advertisement. Date published day Month abbreviation Year <URL>.

Example

WilTel Communications. Advertisement. 10 July 2005 <http://www.msnbc.msn.com/id/3032072/?ta=y>.

Note

^(Note #) Company or product advertised, advertisement, Date published day Month abbreviation Year <URL>.

Example

¹ WilTel Communications, advertisement, 10 July 2005 <http://www.msnbc.msn.com/id/3032072/?ta=y>.

2. Anthology

2a. General

Works Cited Entry

Editor and/or compiler last name, First name Middle initial, ed(s). and/or comp(s). <u>Anthology title</u>. Publication city, State: Publisher, Year published.

Example

Roberts, Edgar V., and Henry E. Jacobs, eds. <u>Literature: An Introduction to Reading and Writing</u>. 5th ed. Upper Saddle River, NJ: Prentice Hall, 1998.

Note

^{Note #} Editor first name Middle initial. Last name, ed. <u>Anthology title</u> (Publication city, State: Publisher, Year published). Page number starts-Ends.

Example

² Edgar V. Roberts, and Henry E. Jacobs, eds. <u>Literature: An Introduction to Reading and Writing</u> (Upper Saddle River, NJ: Prentice Hall, 1998). 120-125.

2b. Previously Independently Published Selection

When the selection you are referencing has already been published independently, be sure to italicize or underline the selection title.

Works Cited Entry

Selection author last name, First name Middle initial. <u>Selection title</u>. Original year published. Trans. Translator first name Middle name Last name. <u>Anthology title</u>. Ed. and/or comp. Editor and/or compiler first name Middle initial. Last name and Second editor and/or compiler first name Middle initial. Last name. Publication city, State: Publisher, Year published. Page number starts-Ends.

Ch. 4

Example

Miller, Arthur. <u>Death of a Salesman</u>. 1949.
<u>Literature: An Introduction to Reading and
Writing</u>. Eds. Edgar V. Roberts and Henry E.
Jacobs. Upper Saddle River, NJ: Prentice
Hall, 1998. 1351-1416.

Note

[Note #] Selection author first name Middle initial. Last
name, <u>Selection title</u>, trans. Translator first name Middle
name Last name, <u>Anthology title</u>, ed. and/or comp.
Editor and/or compiler first name Middle initial. Last
name (Publication city, State: Publisher, Year published)
Page number starts-Ends.

Example

[2] Arthur Miller, <u>Death of a Salesman</u>,
<u>Literature: An Introduction to Reading and
Writing</u>, eds. Edgar V. Roberts and Henry E.
Jacobs (Upper Saddle River, NJ: Prentice Hall,
1998) 1351-1416.

2c.   Never Independently Published Selection

When the selection you are referencing has never been
published independently, be sure to put the selection title
in quotation marks.

Works Cited Entry

Selection author last name, First name Middle initial.
"Selection title." <u>Anthology title</u>. Ed. Editor first name
Middle initial. Last name and Second editor first name
Middle initial. Last name. Publication city, State:
Publisher, Year published. Page number starts-Ends.

Note

[Note #] Selection author first name Middle initial. Last
name, "Selection title," trans. Translator first name
Middle initial. Last name, <u>Anthology title</u>, ed. and/or
comp. Editor and/or compiler first name Middle initial.
Last name (Publication city, State: Publisher, Year
published) Page number starts-Ends.

3.   Blog

3a.   Entry

Works Cited Entry

Author last name, First name Middle initial. "Entry title." Blog title. Blog creation date day Month abbreviation Year. Date accessed day Month abbreviation Year <URL>.

Example

Kipen, David. "Action in the Mid-Atlantic."
    Big Read Blog. 16 Mar. 2007. 8 May 2007
    <http://www.nea.gov/bigreadblog/?m=200703>.

Note

Note # Author first name Middle initial. Last name, "Entry title," Blog title, Blog creation date day Month abbreviation Year. Date accessed day Month abbreviation Year <URL>.

Example

    [3] David Kipen. "Action in the Mid-
Atlantic." Big Read Blog, 16 Mar. 2007. 8 May
2007 <http://www.nea.gov/bigreadblog/
?m=200703>.

3b.   Comment

Works Cited Entry

Poster last name, First name Middle initial (or screen ID). "[Comment title, or first few words,]" Blog comment. Comment date day Month abbreviation Year. "Blog entry title." Blog entry author first name Middle initial. Last name. Blog title. Sponsoring organization. Blog entry date day Month abbreviation Year. Date accessed day Month abbreviation Year <URL with comments in context>.

Example

Chiu, Enzo. "[Comments.]" I agree when you
said "home working is not for everybody".
22 Aug. 2006. "Working from home." Jeffrey
Hill. English Blog. 31 Jan. 2006. 8 May
2007 <http://jeffreyhill.typepad.com/
english/2006/01/dialogpod_1_wor.html
#comments>.

Note

Note # Poster first name Middle initial. Last name (or
screen ID), "[Comment title, or first few words,]" Blog
comment, Comment date day Month abbreviation Year,
"Blog entry title," Blog entry author first name Middle
initial. Last name, Blog title, Sponsoring organization,
Blog entry date day Month abbreviation Year, Date
accessed day Month abbreviation Year <URL with
comments in context>.

Example

³ Enzo Chiu, "[Comments,]" I agree when you
said "home working is not for everybody", 22
Aug. 2006, "Working from home," Jeffrey Hill,
English Blog, 31 Jan. 2006, 8 May 2007
<http://jeffreyhill.typepad.com/
english/2006/01/dialogpod_1_wor.html
#comments>.

4.   Book

4a.   One Author

Works Cited Entry

Author last name, First name Middle initial. <u>Book title</u>.
Ed. Editor first name Middle initial. Last name.
Publication city: Publisher, Year published.

Example

```
Fitzgerald, F. S. Great Gatsby. Ed. Nicholas
     Tredell. New York: Columbia UP, 1997.
```

Note

^{Note #} Author first name Middle initial. Last name, <u>Book title</u>, ed. Editor first name Middle initial. Last name (Publication city: Publisher, Year published) Page number starts-Ends.

Example

```
     ⁴ F. S. Fitzgerald, Great Gatsby, ed.
Nicholas Tredell (New York: Columbia UP, 1997)
91-93.
```

4b.   One Author (Online)

Works Cited Entry

Author last name, First name Middle initial. <u>Book title</u>.
Ed. Editor first name Middle initial. Last name.
Publication city: Publisher, Year published. <u>Site title</u>.
Ed. Site editor first name Middle initial. Last name.
Vers. number. Electronic publication date Day Month
abbreviation Year. Sponsoring organization. Date
accessed day Month abbreviation Year <URL>.

Example

```
Smith, Logan P. Trivia. Ed. Thomas H.
     Salinger. Austin: EBook, 2005. Project
     Gutenberg. Ed. John Ockerbloom. Vers. 3.
     23 Jan. 2005. Project Gutenberg. 17 July
     2005 <http://www.gutenberg.org/dirs/
     etext05/7triv10.txt>.
```

Ch. 4

Note

^{Note #} Author first name Middle initial. Last name, <u>Book title</u>, ed. Editor first name Middle initial. Last name (Publication city: Publisher, Year published), <u>Site title</u>, ed. Site editor first name Middle initial. Last name, vers. number, Electronic publication date day Month abbreviation Year, Sponsoring organization, Date accessed day Month abbreviation Year <URL>.

Example

```
    4 Logan P. Smith, Trivia, ed. Thomas H.
Salinger (Austin: EBook, 2005), Project
Gutenberg, ed. Harold B. Wright, vers. 10, 23
Jan. 2005, 23 Aug. 2005
<http://www.gutenberg.org/dirs/etext05/
7triv10.txt>.
```

4c.   Two Authors

Works Cited Entry

First author last name, First name Middle initial., and Second author first name Middle initial. Last name. <u>Book title</u>. Publication city: Publisher, Year published.

Example

```
Underwood, John, and Ted Williams. Science of
    Hitting. New York: Fireside, 1986.
```

Note

^{Note #} First author first name Middle initial. Last name and Second author first name Middle initial. Last name, <u>Book title</u> (Publication city: Publisher, Year published) Page number starts-Ends.

Example

```
    4 John Underwood and Ted Williams, Science
of Hitting (New York: Fireside, 1986) 83-91.
```

4d.   Group Author

Works Cited Entry

Association, company, or committee. <u>Book title</u>. Ed. Editor first name Middle initial. Last name. Publication city: Publisher, Year published.

Example

United Nations. <u>Basic Facts about the United Nations</u>. Ed. United Nations. New York: United Nations Publications, 2004.

Note

^{Note #} Association, company, or committee, <u>Book title</u>, ed. Editor first name Middle initial. Last name (Publication city: Publisher, Year published) Page number starts-Ends.

Example

⁴ United Nations, <u>Basic Facts about the United Nations</u>, ed. United Nations (New York: United Nations Publications, 2004) 67-71.

4e.   Group Author (Online)

Works Cited Entry

Association, company, or committee. <u>Book title</u>. Ed. Editor first name Middle initial. Last name. Publication city, State: Publisher, Year published. <u>Site title</u>. Ed. Site editor first name Middle initial. Last name. Vers. number. Electronic publication date day Month abbreviation Year. Sponsoring organization. Date accessed day Month abbreviation Year <URL>.

Example

Young Writers Association. <u>Helen of the Old House</u>. Ed. Harold B. Wright. Chicago, IL: EBook, 2004. <u>Project Gutenberg</u>. Ed. John Ockerbloom. Vers. 3. 4 Jan. 2004. Project Gutenberg. 30 Sept. 2004 <http:// www.gutenberg.org/dirs/etext05/ 7hohs10.txt>.

Note

Note # Association, company, or committee, <u>Book title</u>
(Publication city, State: Publisher, Year published), <u>Site</u>
<u>title</u>, ed. Site editor first name Middle initial. Last name,
vers. number, Electronic publication date day Month
abbreviation Year, Sponsoring organization, Date
accessed day Month abbreviation Year <URL>.

Example

⁴ Young Writers Association, <u>Helen of the</u>
<u>Old House</u> (Chicago, IL: EBook, 2004), <u>Project</u>
<u>Gutenberg</u>, ed. Harold B. Wright, vers. 3. 4
Jan. 2004, Project Gutenberg, Project
Gutenberg, 30 Sept. 2004 <http://
www.gutenberg.org/dirs/etext05/7hohs10.txt>.

4f.   Translated

Works Cited Entry

Author last name, First name Middle initial. <u>Book title</u>.
Trans. Translator first name Middle initial. Last name.
Ed. Editor first name Middle initial. Last name.
Publication city: Publisher, Year published.

Example

Saint-Exupèry, Antoine de. <u>Little Prince</u>.
    Trans. Katherine Woods. New York: Harcourt
    Brace and Company, 1943.

Note

Note # Author first name Middle initial. Last name, <u>Book</u>
<u>title</u>, trans. Translator first name Middle initial. Last
name, (Publication city: Publisher, Year published) Page
number starts-Ends.

Example

⁴ Antoine de Saint-Exupèry, <u>Little Prince</u>,
trans. Katherine Woods, (New York: Harcourt
Brace and Compant, 1943) 34-38

5.   Cartoon

When referencing a cartoon from a newspaper, include the newspaper publication city after the publication title in brackets.

Example

Telegram & Gazette [Worcester, MA].

Works Cited Entry

Cartoonist last name, First name Middle initial. "Cartoon title." Cartoon. Publication title Date published day Month abbreviation Year: Page number.

Example

Schulz, Charles M. "Peanuts." Cartoon. Cape
    Cod Times [Hyannis, MA] 14 July 2005: B5.

Note

Note # Cartoonist first name Middle initial. Last name, cartoon, Publication title Date published day Month abbreviation Year: Page number.

Example

⁵ Charles M. Schulz, cartoon, Cape Cod
Times [Hyannis, MA] 14 July 2005: B5.

6. Court Case

Works Cited Entry

Case name. No. Case number. Deciding court name.
Decision date day Month abbreviation Year.

Example

Brown v. Board of Education. No. 347 U.S. 483.
    Supreme Ct. of the US. 17 May 1954.

Note

Note # Case name, no. Case number, Deciding court name,
Decision date day Month abbreviation Year.

Example

    6 Brown v. Board of Education, no. 347 U.S.
483, Supreme Ct. of the US, 17 May 1954.

7. Dictionary

Works Cited Entry

"Defined word." Def. Definition number. <u>Dictionary
title</u>. Ed. Editor first name Middle initial. Last name.
Edition number (2nd, 3rd, 15th, etc) ed. Publication city:
Publisher, Year published.

Example

"Irony." Def. 1. <u>Merriam-Webster's Collegiate
    Dictionary</u>. Ed. Frederick C. Mish. 10th ed.
    Springfield: Merriam-Webster, 2000.

Note

Notet # "Defined word," <u>Dictionary title</u>, Edition date Year
ed.

Example

    7 "Irony," <u>Merriam-Webster's Collegiate
Dictionary</u>, 2000 ed.

8. Dissertation

8a. Published

Works Cited Entry

Author last name, First name Middle initial. <u>Dissertation title</u>. Diss. Institution name, Year accepted. Publication city: Publisher, Year published.

Example

Hall, H.L. <u>Occupational Stress: Type A behavior and perceived control as moderators in the stress process</u>. Diss. U of So. FL, 1990. Tampa: n.p., 1990.

Note

^{Note #} Author first name Middle initial. Last name, <u>Dissertation title</u>, diss., Institution name, Year accepted (Publication city: Publisher, Year published) Page number starts-Ends.

Example

⁸ H. L. Hall, <u>Occupational Stress: Type A behavior and perceived control as moderators in the stress process</u>, diss., U of So. FL, (Tampa: n.p., 1990) 5-12.

Ch. 4

8b.   Unpublished

Works Cited Entry

Author last name, First name Middle initial. "Dissertation title." Diss. Institution name, Year accepted.

Example

Peterson, Ryan J. "Gravitational Anomalies In Deep-Space Bodies." Diss. Boston U, 2003.

Note

Note # Author first name Middle initial. Last name, "Dissertation title," diss. Institution name, Year accepted, Page number starts-Ends.

Example

8 Ryan J. Peterson, "Gravitational Anomalies In Deep-Space Bodies," diss., Boston U, 2003.

9.   E-mail

Works Cited Entry

Author last name, First name Middle initial. "Subject line." E-mail to recipient first name Middle initial. Last name. Message date Day Month abbreviation Year.

Example

Jones, Mark D. "English Paper." E-mail to James Williams. 27 March 1998.

Note

Note # Author first name Middle initial. Last name, "Subject Line," e-mail to Recipient first name Middle initial. Last name, Message date day Month abbreviation Year.

Example

9 Mark D. Jones, "English Paper," e-mail to James Williams, 27 March 1998.

10.   Encyclopedia

Works Cited Entry

Entry author last name, First name Middle initial. "Entry title." Reference work title. Ed. Editor first name Middle initial. Last name. Edition number (2nd, 3rd, 15th, etc) ed. Volume number vol. Publication city: Publisher, Year published.

Example

DeBakey, Michael E. "Heart." World Book Encyclopedia. 9 vols. Chicago: World Book, 1984.

Note

Note # "Entry title," Reference work title, Edition date Year ed.

Example

10 "Heart," World Book Encyclopedia, 1984 ed.

11.   Film

Works Cited Entry

Film title. Dir. Director first name Middle initial. Last name. Narr./Perf. first name Middle initial. Last name. Media form (DVD, video, slide program, laser disc, etc). Distributor name, Year released.

Example

Mary Poppins. Dir. Robert Stevenson. Perf. Julie Andrews. Video. Walt Disney, 1964.

Note

Note # Film title, dir. Director first name Middle initial. Last name, narr./perf. first name Middle initial. Last name, Media form (DVD, video, slide program, laser disc, etc.), Distributor name, Year released.

Example

11 Mary Poppins, dir. Robert Stevenson, perf. Julie Andrews, video, Walt Disney, 1964.

12. Government Publication

12a. Author/Editor/Compiler Unknown

Works Cited Entry

Government name. Agency name. <u>Document title</u>. Department within agency. Publication city: Publisher, Date published Day Month abbreviation Year.

Example

US Govt. Treasury Dept. <u>Treasury Designates Saddam Hussein's Nephews</u>. Terrorism and Financial Security. N.p.: n.p., 21 July 2005.

Note

[Note #] Government name, Agency name, <u>Document title</u> (Publication city: Publishing group, Date published year) Page number starts-Ends.

Example

[12] US Govt., Treasury Dept., <u>Treasury Designates Saddam Hussein's Nephews</u> (n.p., 21 July 2005).

12b. Author/Editor/Compiler Known

Works Cited Entry

Author/editor/compiler last name, First name Middle initial., by, ed., or comp. <u>Document title</u>. Government name. Agency name. Department within agency. Document ID. Publication city: Publisher, Date published day Month abbreviation Year.

Example

Welch, Tom, by, <u>Energy Department Awards $92.5 Million to 19 States to Weatherize Homes of Low-Income Families</u>. US Govt. Dept. of Energy. R-05-194. N.p.: n.p., 18 July 2005.

Note

Note # Author/editor/compiler first name Middle initial.
Last name, by, ed., or comp., Document title,
Government name, Agency name (Publication city:
Publishing group, Date published year) Page number
starts-Ends.

Example

    ¹² Tom Welch, Energy Department Awards
    $92.5 Million to 19 States to Weatherize Homes
    of Low-Income Families, US govt., Dept. of
    Energy (18 July 2005) n. pag.

12c. Online

Works Cited Entry

Author/editor/compiler last name, First name Middle
initial., by, ed., or comp. Document title. Government
name. Agency name. Department within agency.
Document ID. Publication city: Publisher, Date
published day Month abbreviation Year. Site title Ed.
Site editor first name Middle initial. Last name. Vers.
number. Electronic publication date day Month
abbreviation Year. Sponsoring organization. Date
accessed day Month abbreviation Year <URL>.

Example

    Aspey, Susan. Spellings Hails New National
        Report Card Results. US Govt. Dept. of
        Educ. N.p.: n.p., 14 July 2005. Department
        of Education. 26 July 2005
        <http://www.ed.gov/news/pressreleases/2005/
        07/07142005.html>.

Note

Note # Author/editor/compiler first name Middle initial. Last name, by, ed., or comp., <u>Document title</u>, Government name, Agency name (Publication city: Publishing group, Date published Year) <u>Site title</u>, ed. Site editor first name Middle initial. Last name, vers. Version number, Electronic publication date day Month abbreviation Year, Sponsoring organization, Date accessed day Month abbreviation Year <URL>.

Example

```
     12 Susan Aspey, Spellings Hails New
National Report Card Results, US Govt.,
Department of Education (N.p.: n.p., 14 July
2005) Dept. of Educ., 26 July 2005,
<http://www.ed.gov/news/pressreleases/2005/07/
07142005.html>.
```

13.   Interview

13a.   Personal, Telephone, or E-mail

Works Cited Entry

Interviewee last name, First name Middle initial. Personal, telephone, or e-mail interview. Date interviewed first day – Last day Month abbreviation Year.

Example

```
Hall, Alan. Personal interview. 12-13 Mar.
   2002.
```

Note

Note # Interviewee first name Middle initial. Last name, personal, telephone, or e-mail interview, Date interviewed first day – Last day Month abbreviation Year.

Example

```
     13 Alan Hall, personal interview, 12-13
March 2002.
```

13b. Magazine Publication

Works Cited Entry

Interviewee last name, First name Middle initial.
Interview with interviewer first name Middle initial.
Last name. "Interview title." <u>Publication title</u>. Date
published day Month abbreviation Year: Page number
starts-Ends.

Note

^{Note #} Interviewee first name Middle initial. Last name,
interview with Interviewer first name Middle initial.
Last name, "Interview title," <u>Publication title</u> (Date
published day Month abbreviation Year): Page number
starts-Ends.

13c. Book Publication

Works Cited Entry

Interviewee last name, First name Middle initial.
Interview with Interviewer first name Middle initial.
Last name. "Interview title." <u>Book title</u>. Ed./Trans.
Editor/Translator first name Middle initial. Last name.
Publication city: Publisher, Year published. Page
number starts-Ends.

Note

^{Note #} Interviewee first name Middle initial. Last name,
interview with Interviewer first name Middle initial.
Last name, "Interview title," <u>Book title</u>, ed./trans.
Editor/Translator first name Middle initial. Last name
(Publication city: Publisher, Year published) Page
number starts-Ends.

13d. Television

Works Cited Entry

Interviewee last name, First name Middle initial.
Interview with Interviewer first name Middle initial.
Last name. <u>Program name</u>. Broadcasting network. Local
network affiliate, Broadcasting city. Date broadcasted
day Month abbreviation Year.

Note

[Note #] Interviewee first name Middle initial. Last name,
interview with Interviewer first name Middle initial.
Last name, <u>Program name</u>, Broadcasting network, Local
network affiliate, Broadcasting city, Date broadcasted
day Month abbreviation Year.

13e. Radio

Works Cited Entry

Interviewee last name, First name Middle initial.
Interview with Interviewer first name Middle initial.
Last name. <u>Program name</u>. Radio broadcasting network.
Local network affiliate, Broadcasting city. Date
broadcasted day Month abbreviation Year.

Note

[Note #] Interviewee first name Middle initial. Last name,
interview with Interviewer first name Middle initial.
Last name, <u>Program name</u>, Radio broadcasting network,
Local network affiliate, Broadcasting city, Date
broadcasted day Month abbreviation Year.

13f.   Video

Works Cited Entry

Interviewee last name, First name Middle initial.
Interview with Interviewer first name Middle initial.
Last name. <u>Video name</u>. Dir. Director first name Middle
initial. Last name. Videocassette. Producer, Year
produced.

Note

^{Note #} Interviewee first name Middle initial. Last name,
interview with Interviewer first name Middle initial.
Last name, <u>Video name</u>, dir. Director first name Middle
initial. Last name, videocassette, Producer, Year
produced.

14.   Introduction, Foreword, Afterward, or Preface

Format a works cited entry for an Introduction,
Foreword, Afterward, or Preface with the format shown
below.

Works Cited Entry

Part author last name, First name Middle initial. Part
name (Introduction, Foreword, Afterward, or Preface).
<u>Book title</u>. By Book author first name Middle initial Last
name. Ed. Editor first name Middle initial. Last name.
Publication city: Publisher, Date published day Month
abbreviation Year. Page number starts-Ends.

Example

```
Gates, David. Introduction. Sense and
    Sensibility. By Jane Austen. New York:
    Random, 2001. ix.
```

14a.   Introduction

Note

^{Note #} Part author first name Middle initial. Last name, introduction, <u>Book title</u>, by Book author first name Middle initial. Last name, trans. Translator first name Middle initial. Last name (Publication city: Publisher, Date published) Page number starts-Ends.

Example

    ¹⁴ David Gates, introduction, <u>Sense and Sensibility</u>, by Jane Austen (New York: Random House, 2001) ix.

14b.   Foreword

Note

^{Note #} Part author first name Middle initial. Last name, foreword, <u>Publication title</u>, by Book author first name Middle initial. Last name, trans. Translator first name Middle initial. Last name (Publication city: Publisher, Date published) Page number starts-Ends.

14c.   Preface

Note

^{Note #} Part author first name Middle initial. Last name, preface, <u>Publication title</u>, by Book author first name Middle initial. Last name, trans. Translator first name Middle initial. Last name (Publication city: Publisher, Date published) Page number starts-Ends.

14d.   Afterward

Note

^{Note #} Part author first name Middle initial. Last name, afterward, <u>Publication title</u>, by Book author first name Middle initial. Last name, trans. Translator first name Middle initial. Last name, (Publication city: Publisher, Date published) Page number starts-Ends.

15.   Journal Article

Works Cited Entry

Author last name, First name Middle initial. "Article title." Journal name Volume number.Issue number (Date published): Page number starts-Ends.

Example

Sobel, Jordan H. "Money Pumps." Philosophy of Science 68.2(June 2001): 242-257.

Note

Note # Author first name Middle initial. Last name, "Article title," Journal name Volume number.Issue number (Date published): Page number starts-Ends

Example

¹⁵ Jordan H. Sobel, "Money Pumps," Philosophy of Science 68.2 (June 2001): 242-257.

16.   Lecture or Public Address

Works Cited Entry

Speaker last name, First name Middle initial. "Lecture title." Event name. Sponsoring organization, Lecture location building, City. Lecture date day Month abbreviation Year.

Example

Bush, George W. "State of the Union Address." State of the Union Address. US govt., US Capitol, Washington, DC. 2 Feb. 2005.

Note

Note # Speaker first name Middle initial. Last name, "Lecture title," Sponsoring organization, Lecture location, Lecture date day Month abbreviation Year.

Example

¹⁶ George W. Bush, "State of the Union Address," US govt., US Capitol, Washington, DC, 2 Feb. 2005.

17.　Legal Source

Works Cited Entry

Act name. Pub. L. Public law number. Enactment date day Month abbreviation Year. Stat. Statutes at large number.

Note

Note # Act name, pub. l. Public law number, Enactment date day Month abbreviation Year, stat. Statute number.

18.　Letter to the Editor

Works Cited Entry

Writer last name, First name Middle initial. Letter. Publication title Issue number Date published day Month abbreviation Year: Page number starts-Ends.

Example

```
Campenni, Col. William. Letter. Washington
     Times 11 Feb. 2004: n. pag.
```

Note

Note # Writer first name Middle initial. Last name, letter, Publication title Issue number (Year published): Page number starts-Ends.

Example

```
     18 Col. William Campenni, letter,
Washington Times 11 (2004): n. pag.
```

19.   Library Subscription Service

19a.   Periodical

Works Cited Entry

Author last name, First name Middle initial. "Article name." Periodical name Volume number. Issue number (Date published day Month abbreviation Year): Page number starts-Ends. Database name. Service name. Library name, City, State. Date accessed day Month abbreviation Year <URL>.

Example

```
Knox, David. "One-Child Family: A New Life-
    Style." Family Coordinator (1978): n. pag.
    JSTOR. Solomon Baker Library, Waltham, MA.
    26 July 2005 <http://www.jstor.org/search>.
```

Note

Note # Author first name Middle initial. Last name, "Article name," Periodical name Volume number. Issue number (Date published month abbreviation Year): Page number starts-Ends, Database name, Online subscription service, Library name, City, State, Date accessed day Month abbreviation Year <URL>.

Example

```
    19 David Knox, "One-Child Family: A New
Life-Style," Family Coordinator (1978): n.
pag. JSTOR. Solomon Baker Library, Waltham,
MA, 26 July 2005 <http://www.jstor.org/
search>.
```

19b.   Not a Periodical

To cite a source from a library subscription service that is *not* a periodical, cite it as though it were *not* from a database, but add the following information to the end of the citation.

Works Cited Entry

<u>Database name</u>. Service name. Library name, City, State abbreviation. Accessed day Month abbreviation Year <URL>.

Note

<u>Database name</u>, Online subscription service, Library name, City, State, Date retrieved day Month abbreviation Year <URL>.

20. Live Performance

In these citations, `Dir./Cond.` refers to the director or conductor of a live performance. When writing your citation, include the director or conductor as applicable, and indicate who you are citing by including the `Dir./Cond.` (or `dir./cond.` in foot and endnotes) in your citation.

Works Cited Entry

<u>Performance title</u>. By Author (or composer) first name Middle initial Last name. Trans. Translator first name Middle initial. Last name. Dir./Cond. First name Middle initial Last name. Perf. Major performer's first name Middle initial. Last name. Performing company. Theater, City. Date performed day Month abbreviation Year.

Example

```
311 Live. By Nick Hexum. Dir. Seth McHullen.
    Perf. Nick Hexum. 311 Music. Coral Sky,
    West Palm Beach. 9 June 2004.
```

Note

Note # Major performer's first name Middle initial. Last name, perf., <u>Performance title</u>, by Author (or composer) first name Middle initial. Last name, trans. First name Middle initial. Last name, dir./cond. First name Middle initial. Last name, Performing company, Theater, City, Date performed day Month abbreviation Year.

Example

[20] Nick Hexum, perf., 311 Live, by Nick
Hexum, dir. Seth McHullen, 311 Music, Coral
Sky, West Palm Beach, 9 June 2004.

21.   Magazine Article

Exclude volume and issue numbers. To cite non-consecutive page numbers, cite the first page followed by a plus sign.

21a.   General

Works Cited Entry

Author last name, First name Middle initial. "Article title." Magazine name Date published day Month abbreviation Year: Page number starts-Ends.

Example

Kealish, Derek. "Cell Development." Scientific
American 1 July 2005: 21-22.

Note

Note # Author first name Middle initial. Last name, "Article title," Magazine name Date published day Month abbreviation Year: Page number starts-Ends.

Example

[21] Derek Kealish, "Cell Development,"
Scientific American 1 July 2005: 21-22.

21b.   Online

Works Cited Entry

Author last name, First name Middle initial. "Article title." Magazine name Date published day Month abbreviation Year. Date accessed day Month abbreviation Year <URL>.

Ch. 4

Example

Fineman, Howard. "Rove at War." <u>Newsweek</u> 25
    July 2005. 26 July 2005
      <http://global.factiva.com.ezp.bentley.edu/
      en/arch/display.asp>.

Note

Note # Author first name Middle initial. Last name,
"Article title," <u>Magazine name</u> Date published day
Month abbreviation Year, Date accessed day Month
abbreviation Year <URL>.

Example

    [21] Howard Fineman, "Rove at War," <u>Newsweek</u>
25 July 2005, 26 July 2005
<http://global.factiva.com.ezp.bentley.edu/en/
arch/display.asp>.

22.   Map or Chart

Works Cited Entry

<u>Map (or chart) title</u>. Map or chart. Publication city:
Publisher, Year published.

Example

Boston. Map. Denver: Mapquest, 2005.

Note

Note # <u>Map or chart title</u>, map/chart (Publication city:
Publisher, Year published).

Example

    [22] <u>Boston</u>, map (Denver: Mapquest, 2005).

23.   MUD or MOO Posting

Works Cited Entry

Writer last name, First name Middle initial. Online posting. Event date day Month abbreviation Year. Forum title. Date accessed day Month abbreviation Year <URL>.

Example

Fielding, Todd. Online posting. 12 Nov. 2004.
    Healthy World. 21 Dec. 2004
    <http://boards.ign.com/
    message.asp?topic=93331392&replies=0312>.

Note

Note # Writer first name Middle initial. Last name, online posting, Event date day Month abbreviation Year, Forum title, Date accessed day Month abbreviation Year <URL >.

Example

    23 Todd Fielding, online posting. 12 Nov.
2004, Healthy World, 21 Dec. 2004
<http://boards.ign.com/message.asp?
topic=93331392&replies=0312>.

24.   Musical Composition

24a.   Unpublished Score

Works Cited Entry

Composer last name, First name Middle initial. Work title, op. Op. number.

Example

Leo Kemper. Spaceboy, op. 3.

Note

Note # Composer first name Middle initial. Last name, Work title, op. Op number.

Example

    24 Leo Kemper, Spaceboy, op. 3.

24b. Published Score

Works Cited Entry

Composer last name, First name Middle initial. <u>Work title</u>. Year composed. Publication city: Publisher, Year.

Example

Grohl, Dave. <u>In Your Honor</u>. 2005. N.p.: RCA
    Records, 2005.

Note

Note # Composer first name Middle initial. Last name, Work title, Year composed (Publication city: Publisher, Year) Page/Line number starts-Ends.

Example

[24] Dave Grohl, <u>In Your Honor</u>, 2005 (N.p.:
RCA Records, 2005) lines 4-5.

25. Newspaper Article

25a. General

Works Cited Entry

Author last name, First name Middle initial. "Article title." <u>Newspaper title</u> Editorial date published day Month abbreviation Year, Edition ed.: Section page number starts-Ends.

Example

Richardson, Leroy. "Heart Attacks Rising."
    <u>Boston Globe</u> 14 July 2005, 1st ed.: 44-5.

Note

Note # Author first name Middle initial. Last name, "Article title," <u>Newspaper title</u> Date published day Month abbreviation Year: Section letter Page number starts-Ends.

Example

[25] Leroy Richardson, "Heart Attacks
Rising," <u>Boston Globe</u> 14 July 2005: 44-5.

25b. Online

Works Cited Entry

Author last name, First name Middle initial. "Article title." Newspaper title Date published day Month abbreviation Year. Sponsoring organization. Date accessed day Month abbreviation Year <URL>.

Example

```
Greenberger, Scott S. "Romney Vetoes Law on
    Pill, Takes Aim at Roe v. Wade." Boston
    Globe 26 July 2005. 26 July 2005 <http://
    www.boston.com/news/local/massachusetts/art
    icles/2005/07/26/romney_vetoes_law_on_
    pill_takes_aim_at_roe_v_wade/>.
```

Note

[Note #] Author first name Middle initial. Last name, "Article title," Newspaper title Date published day Month abbreviation Year, Date accessed day Month abbreviation Year <URL>.

Example

```
   25 Scott S. Greenberger, "Romney Vetoes Law
on Pill, Takes Aim at Roe v. Wade," Boston
Globe 26 July 2005, 26 July 2005
<http://www.boston.com/news/local/
massachusetts/articles/2005/07/26/romney_
vetoes_law_on_pill_takes_aim_at_roe_v_wade/>.
```

Ch. 4

26. Painting, Sculpture, or Photograph

If the artwork appears in a publication, a book or magazine, you must include that book or magazine's publication information after stating the city where the artwork is located.

Works Cited Entry

Artist last name, First name Middle initial. Artwork title. Art location as museum (or owner), City. Publication name. By Author first name Middle initial. Last name. Publication city: Publisher, Year published. Page, slide, figure, or plate number.

Example

```
Da Vinci, Leonardo. Mona Lisa. Louvre, Paris.
    Mona Lisa's Life. By Samantha Friedman. New
    York: McArthus, 2001. N. pag.
```

Note

Note # Artist first name Middle initial. Last name, Artwork title, Art location as museum (or owner), City. Publication title, by Author first name Middle initial. Last name (Publication city: Publisher, Year published) Page, slide, figure, or plate number.

Example

```
²⁶ Leonardo da Vinci, Mona Lisa, Louvre,
Paris. Mona Lisa's Life, by Samantha Friedman
(New York: McArthus, 2001) n. pag.
```

27. Podcast

Works Cited Entry

"Podcast title." Podcast topic. Relayed day Month abbreviation Year. Accessed day Month abbreviation Year <URL>.

Example

```
"The Detective Police." Charles Dickens crime
    stories. 12 Mar. 2006. 8 May 2007
    <http://www.podlit.com/
    index.php?option=com_content&task=view&id=2
    3&Itemid=43>.
```

Note

"Podcast title," Podcast topic, Relayed day Month abbreviation Year, Accessed day Month abbreviation Year <URL>

Example

```
27 "The Detective Police," Charles Dickens
crime stories, 12 Mar. 2006, 8 May 2007
<http://www.podlit.com/
index.php?option=com_content&task=view&id=23&I
temid=43>.
```

28. Radio or Television Program

When citing a radio or television program, you may encounter different roles that need citing depending on what you are viewing/hearing. Include the director, key performers, narrator, and conductors with their respective abbreviations (Dir., Perf., Narr., Cond.) when appropriate.

Works Cited Entry

"Segment (or episode) title." Program title. By/Dir./Perf./Narr./Host/Cond. First name Middle initial. Last name. Network. Local network affiliate, Broadcast city. Date broadcasted day Month abbreviation Year.

Example
```
"Night to Remember." O.C.. Perf. Peter
    Gallagher, Benjamin McKenzie, Misca Barton,
    et al. FOX. WFXT. 4 Aug. 2005.
```

Note
Note # "Segment (or episode) title," Program title, by/dir./perf./host First name Middle initial. Last name, Network, Local network affiliate, Date broadcasted day Month abbreviation Year.

Example
```
    28 "Night to Remember," O.C., perf. Peter
Gallagher, Benjamin McKenzie, Misca Barton, et
al, FOX, WFXT, 4 Aug. 2005.
```

29. Review

29a. General

Works Cited Entry
Reviewer last name, First name Middle initial. "Review title." Rev. of Work reviewed, by/dir. Author/Director first name Middle initial. Last name. Publication title Date published day Month abbreviation Year: Page number starts-Ends.

Example
```
Henricks, Mark. "Mommy Dearest." Rev. of
    Trillion-Dollar Mom$, by Maria T. Bailey
    and Bonnie W. Ulman. Entrepreneur July
    2005: 20.
```

Note
Note # Reviewer first name Middle initial. Last name, "Review title," rev. of Work reviewed, dir./by Director/Author first name Middle initial. Last name, Publication title Date published day Month abbreviation Year: Page number starts-Ends.

Example
[29] Mark Henricks, "Mommy Dearest," rev. of Trillion-Dollar Mom$, by Maria T. Bailey and Bonnie W. Ulman, Entrepreneur July 2005: 20.

29b.   Online

Works Cited Entry
Reviewer last name, First name Middle initial. "Review title." Rev. of Work reviewed, by/dir. Author/Director first name Middle initial. Last name. Publication title Date published day Month abbreviation Year. Date accessed day Month abbreviation Year <URL>.

Example
Lewis, Anthony. "Privilege and the Press." Rev. of Speaking Freely: Trials of the First Amendment, by Floyd Abrams. New York Review of Books 14 July 2005. 14 July 2005 <http://www.nybooks.com/ articles/18111>.

Note
Note # Reviewer first name Middle initial. Last name, "Review title," rev. of Work reviewed, dir./by Director/Author first name Middle initial. Last name, Publication title Date published day Month abbreviation Year, Date accessed day Month abbreviation Year <URL>.

Example
[29] Anthony Lewis, "Privilege and the Press," rev. of Speaking Freely: Trials of the First Amendment, by Floyd Abrams, New York Review of Books 14 July 2005, 14 July 2005 <http://www.nybooks.com/articles/18111>.

Ch. 4

30.   Sacred Text

Works Cited Entry

Edition title. Editor first name Middle initial. Last name.
Publication city: Publisher, Year.

Example

Holy Bible. New York: National Publishing
    Company, 2005.

Note

Usually sacred texts are cited in works-cited entries
rather than notes.

31.   Thesis

31a.   MA Thesis

Works Cited Entry

Author last name, First name Middle initial. "Thesis
title." MA Thesis. Institution name, Year accepted.

Example

Morales, Reinaldo., Jr. "Nordeste Paintings:
    The case for a pan-archaic American rock
    art tradition." MA Thesis. VA Commonwealth
    U, 1998.

Note

Note # Author first name Middle initial. Last name,
"Thesis title," MA thesis, Institution name, Year
accepted, Page number starts-Ends.

Example

    [31] Reinaldo Morales Jr., "Nordeste
Paintings: The case for a pan-archaic American
rock art tradition," MA thesis, VA
Commonwealth U, 1998, 3-6.

31b.   MS Thesis

Works Cited Entry

Author last name, First name Middle initial. "Thesis title." MS thesis. Institution name, Year accepted.

Example

MacDonald, John. "Stable isotopic and trace
    metal analyses of two Porites Lobata
    colonies - Oahu, Hawaii: implications for
    past seasonal variation and sea surface
    temperatures and anthropogenic effects on
    the reef environment." MS thesis. NY-U at
    Albany, 2005.

Note

[Note #] Author first name Middle initial. Last name, "Thesis title," MS thesis, Institution name, Year accepted, Page number starts-Ends.

Example

[31] John MacDonald, "Stable isotopic and
trace metal analyses of two Porites Lobata
colonies - Oahu, Hawaii: implications for past
seasonal variation and sea surface
temperatures and anthropogenic effects on the
reef environment," MS thesis, NY-U at Albany,
2005, 3-4.

32.   Web Site

32a.   General

Works Cited Entry

Site title. Ed. Editor first name Middle initial. Last name. Date published (or updated) day Month abbreviation Year. Sponsoring organization. Date accessed day Month abbreviation Year <URL>.

Example

CNN. Ed. Marsha Walton. 27 July 2005. Central
    News Network. 27 July 2005
    <http://www.cnn.com/2005/TECH/ space/07/27/
    space.shuttle/index.html>.

Note

Note # <u>Site title</u>, ed. Editor first name Middle initial. Last name, vers. Version number, Electronic publication date day Month abbreviation Year, Sponsoring organization, Sponsoring organization city, Date accessed day Month abbreviation Year <URL>.

Example

```
    32 CNN, ed. Marsha Walton, 27 July 2005,
Central News Network, 27 July 2005
<http://www.cnn.com/2005/TECH/space/07/27/
space.shuttle/index.html>.
```

32b. Web Document

Works Cited Entry

Author last name, First name Middle initial. "Document title." <u>Site title</u>. Ed. Site editor first name Middle initial. Last name. Date published (or updated) day Month abbreviation Year. Sponsoring organization. Date accessed day Month abbreviation Year <URL>.

Example

```
Johns, Julia. "MLA Writing Style." SourceAid.
    10 Nov. 2004. SourceAid, LLC. 29 Jul. 2005
    <http://www.sourceaid.com/writing-style/
    mla.pdf>.
```

Note

Note # Author first name Middle initial. Last name, "Document title," <u>Site title</u>, ed. Site editor first name Middle initial. Last name, vers. Version number, Electronic publication date day Month abbreviation Year, Sponsoring organization, Date accessed day Month abbreviation Year <URL>.

Example

```
    32 Julia Johns, "MLA Writing Style,"
SourceAid, vers.1, 10 Nov. 2004, SourceAid,
LLC, 29 Jul. 2005 <http://www.sourceaid.com/
writing-style/mla.pdf>.
```

5   American Psychological Association

About APA

What is APA?

The information and examples provided in this chapter are consistent with the writing style set forth in the *Publication Manual of the American Psychological Association*, the 5th Edition, as published by the American Psychological Association.   APA is the abbreviation for the American Psychological Association and its writing style.

When should I use APA?

The APA writing style is used for studies in the social sciences—anthropology, communications, economics, education, history, psychology, and sociology among others.

How is APA different?

Unlike most of the other writing styles, foot and endnotes are not major components of an APA paper.   Instead, in-text citations are presented parenthetically, with an author-date system discussed in further detail on page 117.

Composition Layout

Here are some APA guidelines for setting up your paper. See *Figure 5.1* through *Figure 5.4*.

Pagination

Begin pagination with your title page.   Create a right-aligned header with the first few words of your title (or your abbreviated title) and the page number.   Put the same header with the corresponding page number on subsequent pages.

Title page

Double-space the title and center it in the upper half of the title page. On the lines below the title, write your name and institutional affiliation.

Abstract

If you have an abstract, put it on the page after the title page. Center Abstract on the top of the page. The abstract should be a single paragraph that explains the purpose of the paper. It should be no longer than 120 words, and should be in block format.

Chapters

The major sections of a research paper in APA style can be considered "chapters" and each should start on a new page. The *Introduction*, *Method*, *Results*, and *Discussion* portions of your paper could all be considered chapters.

Figures and tables

Add figures (such as charts, graphs, pictures, etc.) and tables (orderly rows and columns of data) into text when relevant. If unessential or distracting, put them in appendixes at the end of the work.

The line *below* each figure should have the label *Figure #.* in italics, followed immediately by a figure description.

The two lines *above* each table should have *Table #* followed by the table description on the line below the table number.

Appendixes

An appendix is a section at the end of a publication which contains information that is helpful, but not essential, to supplement the main text. Create Appendix A, B, C etc. if there is more than one appendix.

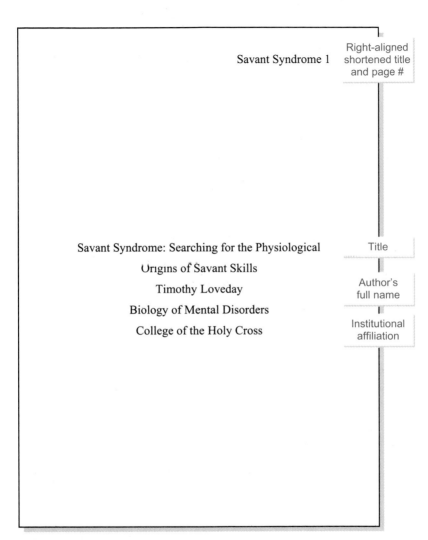

Savant Syndrome 1   Right-aligned shortened title and page #

Savant Syndrome: Searching for the Physiological   Title

Origins of Savant Skills

Timothy Loveday   Author's full name

Biology of Mental Disorders

College of the Holy Cross   Institutional affiliation

Fig. 5.1. Title page layout.

Savant Syndrome 2

Autism is a pervasive developmental disorder

that causes severe deficits in cognitive functioning. It

is a rare disease whose origins still remain a mystery

to researchers. However, even more mysterious is the

disorder called savant syndrome that produces

incredible cognitive talents in autistic individuals,

despite their pervasive disabilities in other areas.

Savant syndrome is a disorder most frequently

seen in autistic individuals, which provides the

individual with incredible mental abilities in a very

limited field. These individuals are otherwise

mentally handicapped to varying degrees, and these

focused talents are obviously not consistent with their

overall mental deficits. Savant skills have been

exhibited by individuals with IQ's ranging from about

40 to above 114 (Treffert & Wallace, 2003). Beate

Hermelin (2001, p.15), a leading expert on savant

syndrome, describes a savant as "a person who,

despite being mentally handicapped and usually also

autistic, nevertheless possesses an outstanding ability

Annotations (right margin):
- Header continues with shortened title & page #
- Double spaced
- Provides background information to introduce reader to topic
- Direct quotation with page number reference

Fig. 5.2. Body layout.

Ch. 5

Savant Syndrome 3

in a specific domain such as art, music, or arithmetic."

Less than one in ten autistic individuals will be

affected by this disorder, and savants are

disproportionately male (Hermelin, 2001). In fact,

there are five to six times more male savants than

female, a fact that will be discussed in more detail

later. Savant syndrome can manifest itself early in life

as a chronic disorder, or it can develop after a brain

disease or injury.

What follows is a presentation and discussion

about the current hypotheses and research regarding

the origins and physiopathology of savant syndrome.

Unfortunately, very little is known about this topic at

this time because most research regarding this

disorder has concentrated on observing *what* savants

do and *how well* they do it rather than *how* and *why*

they do it. Therefore, our current knowledge of the

physiological causes, symptoms, and mechanisms is

still in its infancy and requires a great amount of

further research.

Statistics documented with parenthetical citations

Prepares reader for the body of the paper

Ch. 5

Fig. 5.3. Body layout continued.

Ch. 5

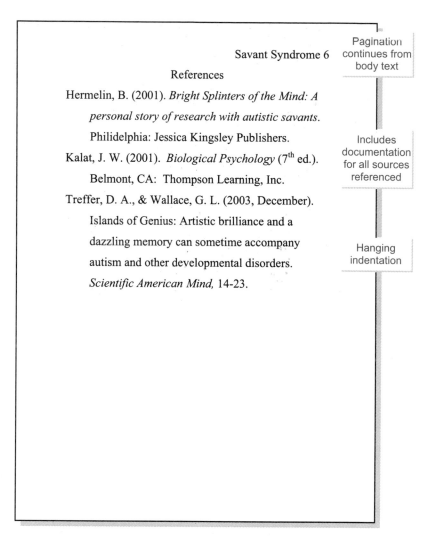

Savant Syndrome 6

Pagination continues from body text

References

Hermelin, B. (2001). *Bright Splinters of the Mind: A*
personal story of research with autistic savants.
Philidelphia: Jessica Kingsley Publishers.

Kalat, J. W. (2001). *Biological Psychology* (7th ed.).
Belmont, CA: Thompson Learning, Inc.

Treffer, D. A., & Wallace, G. L. (2003, December).
Islands of Genius: Artistic brilliance and a
dazzling memory can sometime accompany
autism and other developmental disorders.
Scientific American Mind, 14-23.

Includes documentation for all sources referenced

Hanging indentation

Fig. 5.4. Reference list page layout.

Reference List

For the most part, APA requires that you include a citation in your reference list for each source that you cite in your paper. At the student level, however, if certain teachers require you to include the references you *consulted* in researching your paper, a complete works list can still be called a bibliography in the APA style.

As in all bibliographies and reference lists in any major style, an APA reference list must be all-inclusive with accurate and complete citations.

References Layout

Content
Include the complete and formatted citation information for every source that is referenced in the paper.

Title
Center `References` at the top of your reference list page.

Alignment and indentation
Align the first line of each citation with the left margin. Indent every subsequent line in the citation.

Spacing
Double-space the entire reference list, between and within entries.

Ordering citations
Arrange citations in alphabetical order. If a citation begins with an article (`A`, `An`, or `The`), then use the next word in the citation to place it alphabetically in the reference list.

Pagination
Number the pages of your reference list as a continuation from the text.

Ordering Citations: Special Circumstances

Problematic alphabetization

When arranging your citations alphabetically, keep in mind that the prefixes M', Mc, and Mac should be arranged according to their actual lettering; you should not assume that M', Mc, and Mac all *mean* Mac. McDonough should come before M'Grady. MacGregor comes before McGrath.

When dealing with names that contain prepositions and articles (von, du, de, la), always defer to the rules of the language of origin when attempting to alphabetize them. The *Publication Manual of the American Psychological Association* suggests that researchers refer to *Merriam-Webster's Collegiate Dictionary's* bibliographic section for further help with determining the proper placement of articles and prepositions within names.

When trying to alphabetize works whose authors or titles include Roman numerals, alphabetize according to the letters expressed in the Roman numeral.

Author with multiple publications

If you are working with several publications by the same author, arrange them in your reference list by the date of their publication, from earliest to latest. An article written by Andy Carlsberg in 1998 would precede one written in 2004.

Example

Carlsberg, A. R. (1998).

Carlsberg, A. R. (2004).

Author who has published independent and collaborative work

If you are trying to cite different works by the same author, and one work was produced independently while the other was produced collaboratively, cite the independent work first. In a situation like this, the first part of your citation would resemble the example below, with the collaborative work following the independent one.

Example

Carlsberg, A. R. (1998)

Carlsberg, A. R., & Lieberman, L. A. (1996).

Author who has published collaborative work with several different co-authors

If you are including different works of an author who has collaborated with several different authors, arrange the citations alphabetically by the co-authors' last names.

Example

Carlsberg, A. R. & Frost, T. W. (1996).

Carlsberg, A. R. & Turner, J. D. (1994).

Author with many publication dates from the same year

If you are referencing different works by the same author that have the same publication date, alphabetize the citations by the titles of the articles, unless the articles are part of a series. If the articles are part of a series, order them sequentially and indicate that they are series articles by attaching an alphabetic designator (a lowercase a, b, c, etc.) after the date.

Example

Carlsberg, A. R. (1996a). Title of first article in series.

Carlsberg, A. R. (1996b). Title of second article in series.

Carlsberg, A. R. (1996c). Title of third article in series.

Group authors

If the author of the work is a group or association, include it in the reference list alphabetized by the first significant word of the group title (A, An, or The). Do not use abbreviations for group names in the reference list.

Multiple authors

When a work has up to six authors, it is not necessary to list them according to alphabetical order. List each author's surname, and use only initials to indicate first names. Separate each name from the next with a comma. If the number of authors exceeds six, after listing the first six authors write et al.

Example

DiMare, B. J., Laws, B. C., Poh, T. D., Babcock, M. A., Assaf K. A., Abel, J. D., et al. (2005).

Anonymous authors

When the author is explicitly anonymous, include the work in the reference list by alphabetizing Anonymous as the author name.

No authors

The title, not the date, is the first element of a citation without an author.

Edited book

When you are referencing a book that has an editor but no author, use the editor's name as the primary name in the citation, placing it where the author's name typically is. Signal that you are referring to the editor by adding a parenthetical (Ed. or Eds.) after the editor's name.

Parenthetical Citations

Parenthetical in-text citations in APA use an author-date system, so that the reader immediately knows the source of the information and how current it is.

- In-text citations typically include the author's last name and source publication year. In sources with unknown authors, include the title (shortened if long) and publication year in parentheses after the borrowed information in the text.

- All in-text citations direct the reader to the appropriate source in the Reference List at the end of the text. It is crucial that the spelling and publication information of in-text citations matches up perfectly with the spelling and publication information in your reference list.

- When directly quoting from a source, you must include more specific information regarding where the material is located in the cited text. Include page (p./pp.), paragraph (para.), chapter (chap.), or figure (fig.) number after the publication year in the parenthetical citation.

Author cited within text

When you mention the author in the context of an explanatory sentence about that author's work, create your in-text citation by adding the publication year in parentheses after the author's name is mentioned.

Format

Author last name (Year published) Sentence.

Example

Tejal Patel (2004) theorizes that there is a direct connection between how often a student participates in class discussion and the grade that student earns in the class.

Ch. 5

Author not cited within text

When you reference a work without directly quoting from it or mentioning the author within the sentence, include the author's last name and the publication year in parentheses after the sentence.

Format

Sentence (Author last name, Year published).

Example

There is a correlation between a student's active participation in a class and the grade that he or she will earn in that class (Patel, 2004).

Direct quotation

When you insert a direct quotation from your source into your paper, include the author's last name, the year published, and the page number where you found the quoted section.

Format

Sentence (Author last name, Year published, p. Page number(s)).

Example

"There is a correlation between a student's participation in class, how active he or she is in class discussions, and the grade that the student will earn" (Patel, 2004, p. 2).

Parenthetical Citations: Special Circumstances

In-text citation when the work has up to six authors

When the work you are referencing has up to six authors, include them all in the paper's first citation. In subsequent citations, cite only the first author mentioned in your reference list, followed by et al..

First citation

Example

DiMare, Laws, Poh, Babcock, and Assaf (2005) found that mood affects the listener's music preference.

Example

Studies find that mood affects the listener's music preference (DiMare, Laws, Poh, Babcock, Assaf, 2005).

Subsequent citations

Example

Laws et al. (2005) found that mood affected the listener's music preference.

Example

Studies find that mood affected the listener's music preference (Laws et al., 2005).

In-text citation with more than six authors

When the work you are referencing has six or more authors, you only have to cite the last name of the first author and include `et al.` in the first (and all following) in-text citations.

In-text citations for secondary sources

When citing a secondary source in your text, refer to the original work to which the secondary source refers and include the secondary source's citation in your reference list.

Notes

Students typically use parenthetical in-text citations when referencing materials in the body of their text, but they can also use footnotes. Content and copyright permission footnotes are common in professional APA style publications. Content footnotes supplement information in the text and copyright footnotes give credit to the source of information included in the text.

Understanding APA Terminology

In APA citations, there are certain words you should use to explain publication dates, source types, and people. There are also some terms that you must abbreviate. See Tables 5.1-4 for examples.

Publication Cities

When citing any of the cities listed below in a citation, do not include the state, province, or country.

Baltimore	New York	Paris	Amsterdam
Boston	Philadelphia	Jerusalem	Rome
Chicago	San Francisco	London	Stockholm
Los Angeles	Milan	Tokyo	Moscow
Vienna			

Do not give the name of the state if it is included in a university or institution name.

Publication dates

Table 5.1

Abbreviations for Missing Information

Expression	Description
(in press).	Include this into your citation in lieu of a publication date when the work you are citing has been accepted for publication but has not been printed yet. Though you might know when the work is supposed to be published, never write a publication date until the work is officially published.
(n.d.).	Use this abbreviation in your citation when no date for the work you are citing is available.

Media descriptions

When looking at the citation formats later in this chapter, remember that information in brackets about the source type is essential to include in your citation right after the title.

Table 5.2

Descriptions for Cited Media Types

Expression		
[Abstract]	[Data file]	[Msg]
[Brochure]	[Letter to the editor]	[Television series]
[CD]	[Monograph]	[Special issue]
[Computer software]	[Motion picture]	[Videotape]

People Indicators

Your reader must be able to immediately recognize the roles of people included in your citations. Without certain indicators, it would be hard for a reader to differentiate whether the name in a citation refers to the author of the work, the editor, the translator, or the director.

Table 5.3

Role Designators of People in Citations

Common Indicators	Meaning
(Ed.) or (Eds.)	Editor or Editors
(Trans.)	Translator
(Speaker)	Speaker of Audio Recording
(Producer)	Producer of Audiovisual Media
(Writer)	Writer of Audiovisual Media
(Director)	Director of Audiovisual Media

Citation Formats

Before creating your APA citations, make sure you have looked over the *Understanding APA Terminology* section. Also, please note that if the author is also the publisher use the term `Author` in place of the publisher name.

If APA has not specified a citation format for the source you are citing, use citation formats for similar source types as models to cite the source.

0. Multiple Authors and Editors

To properly format multiple authors and editors, refer to *Ordering Citations: Special Circumstances* on page 114.

1. Anthology

Reference

Editor last name, First initial. Middle initial. (Ed.). (Year published). *Anthology title*. Publication city, State: Publisher.

Example

```
Eisner, W. J. (Ed.). (2003). Mirrors of self
    and world: The psychology of visual art: an
    anthology and study guide. Stamford, CT:
    Thomson Learning Custom Publishing.
```

2. Blog

Reference

Author last name, First initial. Middle initial. (Posting year, Month Day). Entry title. Blog title. Retrieved month Day, Year, from Website sponsor: URL

Example

```
Haegele, K. (2007, March 15). Dr Freud will
    see you now Mr. Hitler. Retrieved June 3,
    2007, from Medical Humanities Society:
    http://medhum.blogspot.com/
    2007_03_01_archive.html
```

Ch. 5

3.   Book

3a.   General

Reference

Author last name, First initial. Middle initial. (Year published). *Book title*. (Edition number ed., Vol. Volume #, p./pp. Page number starts-Ends). In Editor first initial. Middle initial. Last name (Ed.), Publication city, State: Publisher.

Example

Vasta, R. (1992). *Six theories of child development: Revised formulations and current issues*. (Vol. 1, pp. 54-72). London: Jessica Kingsley Publishers.

3b.   Online

Reference

Author last name, First initial. Middle initial. (Year published). *Book title*. (Vol. Volume #, p./pp. Page number starts-Ends). In Editor first initial. Middle initial. Last name (Ed.), Publication city, State: Publisher. Retrieved month Day, Year, from URL

Example

Van Evra, J. (1990). *Television and child development*. (pp. 190-197). Hillsdale, NJ: Lawrence Erlbaum Associates. Retrieved March 24, 1998, from www.questia.com

3c.   Article or Chapter in Edited Book

Reference

Author last name, First initial. Middle initial. (Year published). Article or chapter title. In Editor first initial. Middle initial. Last name (Ed.), *Book title* (Vol. Volume #, p/pp. Page number starts-Ends). Publication city, State: Publisher.

Example

```
Kieff, J. & Wellhousen, K. (2000).
   Developmental expectations of infants and
   toddlers during block play. In A. Ferraro
   (Ed.), A constructive approach to block
   play in early childhood. (pp. 66-77),
   Clifton Park, NY: Thomson Delmar Learning.
```

3d.   Article or Chapter in Edited Book (Online)

Reference

Author last name, First initial. Middle initial. (Year published). Article or chapter title. In Editor first initial. Middle initial. Last name (Ed.), *Book title* (Vol. Volume #, p./pp. Page number starts-Ends). Publication city, State: Publisher. Retrieved month Day, Year, from URL

4.   Computer Software

Reference

Author last name, First initial. Middle initial. (Year published). Software title (Version version #) [Computer software]. Publication city, State: Publisher.

Example

```
Fox, T. (2004). SourceAid (Version 1.0)
   [Computer software]. Boston: SourceAid,
   LLC.
```

Ch. 5

5.   Conference Proceedings

Reference

Author last name, First initial. Middle initial. (Year published). Article title. In Editor first initial. Middle initial. Last name (Ed.), *Proceeding title.* (p./pp. Page number starts-Ends). Publication city, State: Publisher.

6.   Database Article

Reference

Author last name, First initial. Middle initial. (Date published Year, Month Day). Article title. *Source name, Volume or issue #,* Page number starts-Ends. Retrieved month Day, Year, from Database name (Document number)

Example

Peleg, O. (2005, March). The relation between differentiation and social anxiety: What can be learned from students and their parents?. *The American Journal of Family Therapy, 33,* 167-184. Retrieved May 28, 2005, from infotrac.com (A13056916).

7.   Dissertation Abstract

7a.   General

Reference

Author last name, First initial. Middle initial. (Year published). Dissertation title (Doctoral dissertation, Institution, Date accepted month Day, Year). *Dissertation Abstracts International, Volume #,* Page number starts-Ends. (UMI No. Number).

Example

King, C.A. (1972). An investigation of selected associations between personality traits and the human muscular-skeletal structure (Doctoral dissertation, University of Miami, 1972). *Dissertation Abstracts International, 33,* 2713A-2714A. (UMI No.72-31,912).

7b.   Online

Reference

Author last name, First initial. Middle initial. (Year published). Dissertation title (Doctoral dissertation, Institution, Date accepted month Day, Year). *Dissertation Abstracts International, Volume #,* Page number starts-Ends. Abstract retrieved month Day, Year, from URL

Example

Krepack, A.F. (1980). An exploratory study into the 'functional unity' theory: Respiration and personality (Doctoral dissertation, California School of Professional Psychology, Berkeley, 1980). *Dissertation Abstracts International, 40,* 3404B. Abstract retrieved April 20, 1995, from http://www.orgonelab.org

Ch. 5

7c.   Unpublished

Reference

Author last name, First initial. Middle initial. (Year published). *Dissertation title*. Unpublished doctoral dissertation, University, City, State.

8.   Dictionary of Encyclopedia

Reference

Lead editor last name, First initial. Middle initial. (Ed.) (Year published) Book title. (Edition number ed., Vols. Volume number). Publication city, State: Publisher.

9.   Journal Article

9a.   General

Reference

Author last name, First initial. Middle initial. (Year published). Article title. *Journal title, Volume* #(Issue #), Page number starts-Ends.

Example

Reddy, V. et al. (2002). Sharing humour and laughter in autism and Down's syndrome. *British Journal of Psychology, 93*(2), 219-43.

9b.   Online

Reference

Author last name, First initial. Middle initial. (Year published). Article title. *Journal title, Volume* #(Issue #), Page number starts-Ends. Retrieved month Day, Year, from URL

Example

Richardson, K. (2001). Evolving explanations of Development. *American Journal of Psychology, Volume 114*(1), 135-145. Retrieved January 4, 2003, from http://www.press.uillinois.edu/journals/ ajp/ajpsearch.php

10.   Magazine Article

10a.   General

Reference

Author last name, First initial. Middle initial. (Date published year, Month Day). Article title. *Magazine title, Volume* #, Page number starts-Ends.

Example

Dickinson, A. (2000, January 31). Bad boys rule: A new study shows some of the most popular kids in school are "extremely antisocial". *Time Magazine, 155,* 77-78.

10b.   Online

Reference

Author last name, First initial. Middle initial. (Date published year, Month Day). Article title. *Magazine name, Volume* #, Page number starts-Ends. Retrieved month Day, Year, from URL

Ch. 5

Example

Martin, E. W. (2001, March). Emotional eating.
Psychology Today, 34, 20. Retrieved May 2,
2001, from http://cms.psychologytoday.com/
articles/pto-21.html

11.   Motion Picture

Reference

Producer last name, First initial. Middle initial.
(Producer), & Director last name, First initial. Middle
initial. (Director). (Year released). *Movie title* [Motion
picture]. Country produced: Studio name.

Example

Guber, P. (Producer), & Levinson, B.
(Director). (1988). *Rain man* [Motion
picture]. United States: Simon and Goodman
Picture Company Productions.

12.   Music Recording

Reference

Music author last name, First initial. Middle initial.
(Copyright date). Song title. Recorded by First initial.
Last name if different from author. On *Album title*
[Medium type i.e. CD]. Distribution city, State: Label
name. (Date recorded month Day, Year if different from
copyright date)

Example

McLean, D. (1990). American pie. On *American
pie* [CD]. Los Angeles: Capitol Records.

13.   Newspaper Article

13a.   General

Reference

Author last name, First initial. Middle initial. (Date published year, Month Day). Article title. *Newspaper name*. p./pp. Page number starts-Ends.

Example

Stengle, J. (2005, July 26). Exercise won't stall aging, study says. *The Boston Globe*. p. A3.

13b.   Online

Reference

Author last name, First initial. Middle initial. (Date published year, Month Day). Article title. *Newspaper name*. p./pp. Page number starts-Ends. Retrieved month Day, Year, from URL

Example

Nagourney, E. (2005, February 15). Health and happiness aren't always linked. *The New York Times*. F7. Retrieved August 12, 2002, from www.infotrac.com

14.   Online Periodical Article

If you include the URL address in your citation, you do not need to specify [Electronic Version] after the article title.

Reference

Author last name, First initial. Middle initial. (Date published year, Month Day). Article title [Electronic version]. *Periodical name, Volume number* (Issue number), Page number starts-Ends. Retrieved month Day, Year, from URL

Example

```
Lukatela, G. & Turvey, M. T. (1998). Science
    watch: Reading in two alphabets. The
    American Psychologist, 53(9), 1057.
    Retrieved March 2, 1999, from
    http://www.questia.com/
    PM.qst?a=o&d=96504745
```

15.   Online Posting

Provide a screen name if you do not know the author's real name.

Reference

Author last name, First initial. Middle initial. (Date published year, Month Day). String title [Msg Message number]. Message posted to URL

Example

```
Fielding, T. (2004, November 12). A healthy
    world [Msg 21]. Message posted to
    http://boards.ign.com/
    message.asp?topic=93331392&replies=0312
```

Ch. 5

16.   Personal Communication

You should not cite personal communication sources in your reference list because your audience cannot recover information that you acquire through letters, memos, and some electronic communication. You do, however, have to cite personal communication sources in your text.

17.   Podcast

Reference

Producer last name, First initial. Middle initial. (Producer) & Presenter last name, First initial. Middle initial. (Presenter). (Publication year, Month Day). *Podcast title* [Podcast type]. Publication country: Distributor. Retrieved month Day, Year, from URL

Example

Grothe D.J. (Producer) & Hecht J. M. (Presenter). (2007, May 25). *The happiness myth* [Science and medicine]. Amherst, New York: Center for Inquiry. Retrieved June 3, 2007, from iTunes Music Store

18.   Review

Reference

Author last name, First initial. Middle initial. (Date published Year, Month Day). Review title [Review of *medium reviewed*]. Publication title, Volume number, Page number starts-Ends.

Example

Coy, P. (2005, March 14). Energy crisis? Phooey. [Review of the book *The bottomless well*]. BusinessWeek, 23.

19.   Sound Recording

Reference

Speaker last name, First initial. Middle initial. (Speaker). (Year recorded). *Recording title* [Medium type]. Distribution city, State: Distributor name.

Example

Shepard, K., Young, A., & Carson, C. (Speaker). (2001). *A call to conscience: The landmark speeches of Dr. Martin Luther King, Jr.* [Audio CD]. Time Warner Audio Books.

20.   Technical or Research Report

20a.   General

Reference

Report author (Year published). *Report title* (Report number). Publication city, State: Organization.

Example

Unifem (2006). *Report of the United Nations Development Fund for Women* (A/HRC/4/069, E/CN.6/2007/6). New York: Unifem Headquarters.

20b.   Private Organization Report

Reference

Organization name. (Date published Year, Month Day). *Report title* (Document number). Publication city, State: Publisher.

Example

Data Display Products. (2004, May 29). *Financial recovery* (2201). Atlanta, GA: Hill Publishing.

20c. National Technical Information Service Report

Reference

Report author last name, First Initial. Middle Initial. (Year published). *Report title*. Publication city, State: Organization. (NTIS No. Report number)

Example

Bavelier, D. (2006). *Video Games as a Tool to Train Cognitive Skills*. NY: Rochester University. (Final Rept. 30 NTIS Order No. ADA444148)

20d. Educational Resources Information Center Report

Reference

Report author last name, First Initial. Middle Initial. (Year published). *Report title* (Report No. Report number). Publication city, State: Organization. (ERIC Document Reproduction service No. Eric number)

Example

Clabaugh, A. A. & Clabaugh, G. K. (2005) *Bad or Sour Pickles? Fundamental Attribution Error and the Columbine Massacre*. Bloomington, IN: Educational Horizons (ERIC Document Reproduction Service No.EJ685028)

21. Television

21a. Broadcast

Reference

Producer last name, First initial. Middle initial. (Executive producer). (Date aired year, Month Day). *Program title* [Television broadcast]. Production city, State: TV network or service.

Example

Rodriguez, R. R. (Executive producer). (2004, April 12). *Sea lions* [Television broadcast]. San Francisco, CA: Animal Planet.

21b. Series

Reference

Producer last name, First initial. Middle initial. (Producer). (Year produced). *Series name* [Television series]. Production city, State: TV network or service.

Example

Blutman, M. & Busgang, H. (Producers). (1993). *Boy meets world* [Television series]. Burbank, CA: ABC.

21c. Series Episode

Reference

Writer last name, First initial. Middle initial. (Writer), & Director last name, First initial. Middle initial. (Director). (Year produced). Episode title [Television series episode]. In Producer first initial. Middle initial. Last name (Producer), *Series name*. Production city, State: TV network or service.

Example

Kelly, A. (Writer), & Trainer, D. (Director). (1993). Father knows less [Television series episode]. In M. Blutman & H. Busgang (Producers), *Boy meets world*. Burbank, CA: ABC.

22.   Translation

22a.   General

Reference

Author last name, First initial. Middle initial. (Year published). *Book title*. (Vol. Volume number). In Editor first initial. Middle initial. Last name (Ed.), (Translator first initial. Middle initial. Last name, Trans.). Publication city, State: Publisher. (Original work published Year, Month Day)

Example

Nurbakhsh, J. (1992). *The psychology of sulfism*. (T. Graham, Trans.). Khaniqahi Nimatullahi Pubns (Original work published 1993)

22b.   Online

Reference

Author last name, First initial. Middle initial. (Year published). *Book title*. (Vol. Volume number). In Editor first initial. Middle initial. Last name (Ed.), (Translator first initial. Middle initial. Last name, Trans.). Publication city, State: Publisher. (Original work published Year, Month Day) Retrieved Month Day, Year, from URL

Example

Rand, B. (2004). *The classical psychologists: Selections illustrating psychology from Anaxagoras to Wundt*. (W. Alexander, Trans.). Berkeley, CA: University Press of the Pacific. (Original work published 1912) Retrieved August 8, 2004, from www.questia.com

Ch. 5

6 Chicago Manual of Style

About CMS

What is CMS?

The information and examples provided in this chapter are consistent with the writing style set forth in the *Chicago Manual of Style* writing manual, 15th Edition and Turabian's *A Manual for Writers of Research Papers, Theses, and Dissertations,* 7th edition, both published by the University of Chicago Press. CMS is a writing style that originated in 1890 when it was first used by students at the University of Chicago.[2]

When should I use CMS?

The CMS writing style is used in the humanities and history disciplines, as well as in some natural and physical sciences.

How is CMS different?

CMS is known as one of the most simplistic and concise means of citation. Like MLA, the CMS style focuses on citing information about the author, rather than the date.

The CMS documentation system has two citation styles, author-date and notes and bibliography. The author-date style is often used in the humanities and some social sciences, while the notes and bibliography style is typically used in the natural and physical sciences. In the author-date style, parenthetical citations refer readers to the bibliography to get complete source information. In the notes and bibliography style, complete

---

[2] The Chicago Manual of Style - About the Manual, 2005, The University of Chicago, Chicago, 28 July 2005 <http://www.chicagomanualofstyle.org/about.html>.

source information can appear in footnotes or endnotes, as well as in the bibliography.

Composition Layout

While CMS specifies some formatting and layout requirements for journal publications, it does not provide complete guidelines for paper formats at the high school and college level. Be sure to talk to your teacher or professor for his or her formatting preferences. Refer also to *Figure 6.1* through *Figure 6.5* for further help with formatting your research paper.

Font

Use 12 point Times New Roman font for the body of the text and 10 point Times New Roman font for notes.

Margin

Use a 1 inch margin around each page.

Pagination

Begin numbering pages in the footer on the first page of text, excluding the title page.

Title

Center the title on the first page of full text, 2 inches below the top of the page.

Title page

Center the title. Put your abstract (a short summary of the main points discussed in your paper) a few lines below the title. After the abstract, include your name, the department name, course name and number, and the date in Month Day, Year format.

Tables

Put the number and a title on the line above the table, with the word Table, followed by the table number, followed by a period as in Table #. Put the source information below the table, as shown in the sample table below.

Table #. Title

	Insert table here.	

Source: Data from

Fig. 6.1. Format to include a table in your research.

Number tables separately from figure numbers. Table numbers should be consecutive in the same order as they appear in the text If you have several tables and many chapters, however, number your tables in this double numeration format: Chapter #.Table #. The second table in the third chapter would be 3.2.

Figures

On the line *below* a figure, label the figure number and the title with the format Figure #. Title.. If you only have a few figures, do not number them. Put any captions in a smaller typeface than that of your body text.

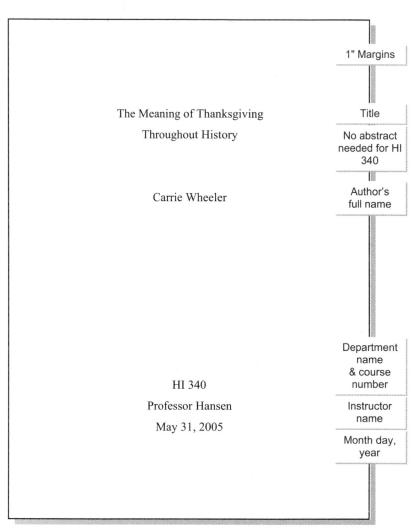

Fig. 6.2. Title page layout.

Thanksgiving Day, as represented in the media, is often stereotyped as a day that serves to commemorate a turkey feast shared peacefully by English colonists, or Pilgrims, and the Wampanoag Indians in 1621. Unbeknownst to many Americans and inaccurately portrayed in various commercial representations, the real "First Thanksgiving" did not occur until centuries after the pilgrims' and Indians' grand meal. The description of the Pilgrims' and Indians' feast that was recovered by Americans from British looters in *Mourt's Relation: A Journey of the Pilgrims at Plymouth* did, however, partially inspire what came to be the real "First Thanksgiving." While focusing on how Thanksgiving's meaning has diversified with time, scholars may discount the similarities between Thanksgivings of past and present.

The article "The National Day of Mourning" featured on Pilgrim Hall Museum's website is just one example that explains a variety of perspectives of

1

1" Margins

Introduction

Cites primary source

Thesis Statement

Cites secondary source

Pagination begins

Fig. 6.3. Body layout.

Ch. 6

Thanksgiving that have developed throughout history.
It explains, for instance, how Thanksgiving came to
be a National Day of Mourning for many Native
Americans in 1970. By showing this somber
viewpoint, it illustrates a perspective of Thanksgiving
that has developed since 1782 when the United States
Congress foresaw it as a potential holiday for
"national happiness."[1] "The National Day of
Mourning" also indicates that some Americans have a
more positive view of Thanksgiving. These
Americans, according to the article, view
Thanksgiving as a reason to hope that the "respect that
was possible once [between the Pilgrims and
Wampanoag Indians], if only for a brief span of a
single generation...may again be possible some day."[2]
This viewpoint also conceptually implies that
Thanksgiving's significance has diversified beyond its
original purpose as "a day of solemn Thanksgiving."[3]
While it is evident that Thanksgiving's purpose has
diversified with societal changes, it is left unclear

2

Times New
Roman

12 pt font

Double spaced

Fig. 6.4. Body layout continued.

Notes

First line of
note indented
½ "

1. John Hanson, "Proclamation," "The Learning Page," Library of Congress, <http://memory.loc.gov/learn/lessons/constitu/thanks.html> (accessed May 30, 2005).

Single spaced
within notes

2. "The National Day of Mourning," "Pilgrim Hall Museum," <http://www.pilgrimhall.org/daymourn.htm> (accessed May 30, 2005).

Double spaced
between notes

3. Hanson

4. *Mourt's Relation: A Journal of the Pilgrims at Plymouth* ed. Dwight B. Heath (Bedford, MA: Applewood Books, 1986), 44.

5. Joy Hakim, *Making Thirteen Colonies* (New York: Oxford University Press, Inc., 2003).

6. Caleb Johnson, "The Pilgrims' 1621 Thanksgiving," "Caleb Johnson's MayflowerHistory.com," MayflowerHistory, <http://members.aol.com/calebj/thanksgiving.html> (accessed May 29, 2003).

6

Pagination
continued

Fig. 6.5. Endnotes.

Ch. 6

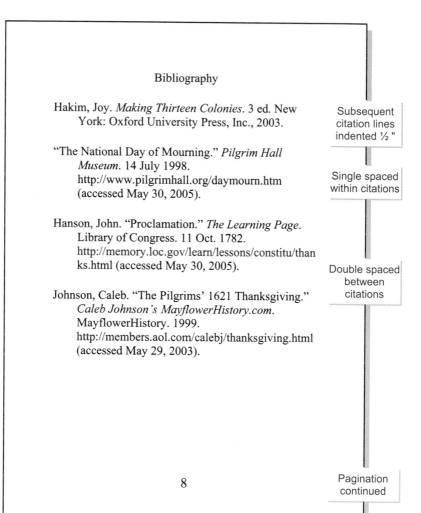

Bibliography

Hakim, Joy. *Making Thirteen Colonies*. 3 ed. New York: Oxford University Press, Inc., 2003.

"The National Day of Mourning." *Pilgrim Hall Museum*. 14 July 1998. http://www.pilgrimhall.org/daymourn.htm (accessed May 30, 2005).

Hanson, John. "Proclamation." *The Learning Page*. Library of Congress. 11 Oct. 1782. http://memory.loc.gov/learn/lessons/constitu/thanks.html (accessed May 30, 2005).

Johnson, Caleb. "The Pilgrims' 1621 Thanksgiving." *Caleb Johnson's MayflowerHistory.com*. MayflowerHistory. 1999. http://members.aol.com/calebj/thanksgiving.html (accessed May 29, 2003).

Subsequent citation lines indented ½ "

Single spaced within citations

Double spaced between citations

8

Pagination continued

Fig. 6.6. Bibliography.

Bibliography

A bibliography, sometimes called Sources Consulted, is the last page(s) accompanying a research paper. It lists all of the publication information for each documented or referenced source that contributes to your work.

As in all bibliographies and reference lists in any major style, a standard CMS bibliography must be all-inclusive with accurate and complete citations. You may also consider alternative bibliography styles, such as those explained later in this section.

Bibliography Layout

Contents
Include each source that you consulted during research.

Title
Center `Bibliography` 1 inch below the top of the page.

Alignment and indentation
Align the first line of each citation with the left margin. Indent subsequent lines 5 spaces.

Spacing
Double-space between entries but single-space within entries.

Ordering citations
Arrange citations in alphabetical order. If a citation begins with an article (`The`, `A`, or `An`), then use the next word in the citation to place it alphabetically in the bibliography. For more specifics, see *Ordering Citations: Special Circumstances* on page 150.

Pagination
Number the pages of the bibliography as a continuation from the text.

Choosing the Right Kind of Bibliography

Although most student researchers follow the basic bibliography format described in the previous section, you should recognize that other bibliography formats are available that may be more suitable for your research needs. The other bibliography formats include annotated bibliographies, single-author bibliographies, divided bibliographies, selected bibliographies, and reference lists. This section will focus on the latter three types.

Annotated bibliography

An annotated bibliography is a bibliography with explanations accompanying the citations.

Reasons for Use

- Document something about the source for a reader or for yourself

- Indicate how each source contributes to your research

- Discover if you have gathered enough research materials to support your thesis

- Force you to identify how research materials are relevant

Method

Add annotations (comments regarding sources) one line below each citation in your bibliography. SourceAid's Citation Builder software can help you to format the annotations. If you want to annotate by hand, use the following format and guidelines.

Spacing

Single-space annotations just as the bibliographic citations are single spaced within entries and double spaced between entries.

Indentation

Indent the annotation from the bibliography to allow the reader to differentiate between the bibliography and the annotation.

Format

Bibliographic information.

Annotation.

Single-author bibliography

A single-author, or Published Works of Author, bibliography lists one author's publications chronologically.

Reasons for Use

- Your sources are authored by one person, so using the typical bibliography format where citations are alphabetized by author name would not be useful.

- Your sources are authored by one person and it is beneficial to view the sources by publication date.

Method

- Title the bibliography Published Works of Author Full Name.

- Arrange your sources chronologically by publication date.

- Group your citations by date if there are numerous publications in each year.

Divided bibliography

A divided bibliography groups sources categorically.

Reasons for Use

- Organize research materials in a layout that is more logical to the reader than the standard alphabetical order by author last name

- Categorically distinguish source types consulted during research if it will not interfere with the reader's ability to cross reference citations between the notes and the bibliography

Ch. 6

- Source types are important to the nature of your paper's discussion, or to the reader's understanding of your perspective

Method

- Divide the works that you have cited (as opposed to consulted) into categories.

- Describe your reasoning for dividing your bibliography into the chosen categories in the page heading.

- Alphabetize sources within the categories.

Ordering Citations: Special Circumstances

CMS bibliographic citations are traditionally arranged in alphabetical order by the author's last name, but citations can also be ordered chronologically (in single-author citation lists) or categorically. Citation categories can be physical form (books, manuscripts, videos, etc...), topic, or degree of originality (primary/secondary/tertiary levels).

Author who has published independent and collaborative work

A single-author book should precede a multi-author book with the same author name.

Example

Bibliography

Pault, Tabitha Q. *Cognitive Development of Today's Leaders.* Current Sociological Developments. Vol. 2 of *Cognitive Development of Today's Leaders* Edited by Francis Renoir. New York: Yoiler Inc., 2003.

Pault, Tabitha Q, and Robert Craig. *Uniting Communities for Co-operative Advancement.* Current Sociological Developments. Vol. 2 of *Uniting Communities for Co-operative Advancement* Edited by Francis Renoir. New York: Yoiler Inc, 2003.

Author who has published collaborative work with several different co-authors

When two entries have the same author, but have different co-authors, alphabetize them by the co-authors' last names.

Example

Bibliography

Chan, Anita, Graeme Gill, Robert F. Miller, Mark Selden, Gordon White, and Wong Siu-Iun. *China After Socialism: In the Footsteps of Eastern Europe or East Asia?*. Edited by Barrett L. McCormick, Paul Bowles, and Jonathan Unger M.E. Sharpe, 1996.

Chan, Anita, Richard Madsen, and Jonathan Unger. *Chen Village Under Mao and Deng*. Berkeley and Los Angeles: University of California Press, 1992.

Text Citations

This section explains how to use note and parenthetical citations in specific circumstances.

Note Citations

Use a superscript to refer to a note containing a source's publication information. The first text citation is superscripted with a [1], the second text citation is superscripted with a [2], and the numbering continues sequentially. Superscripts can be placed after any punctuation except a dash.

If the statement in the text you want to cite comes from several sources, include the publication information for each of its sources in a single note. Use semi-colons to separate the citations in the note.

See the *Endnotes* section on page 156 for additional information.

Format

Sentence.^{N}

N = the sequential number of the text citation

Example

Blogs and alternative news sites' content informs defined psychographic sectors of the public about specific story angles not available in mainstream media.[15]

Note: Be aware that if you use notes to cite your sources you are not committed to using notes in subsequent references to the sources. See *Parenthetical citation to a note* in the next section when referencing a note citation parenthetically.

Parenthetical Citations

In some circumstances, particularly when you exclude notes from your work, you may choose to cite sources within the body of your text. Parenthetical citations are more commonly used in the CMS author-date documentation style than in bibliography and note style. The following guidelines and examples will help you to incorporate parenthetical citations into your text.

Parenthetical citation to a note

If full publication information for the source is given in a note, subsequent references may be cited in the text. The note must indicate that subsequent references to this source will be cited in the text.

Format

"Quoted sentence" (Partial publication information).

Example

Although historical documents suggest that its society had prejudices, "New Philadelphia was the first example of bi-racial cooperation in the United States before the Civil War" (Mackenzie).

Complete citation following short quotation

Full publication information can be included as a parenthetical citation after a quoted sentence. Note that the period appears after the citation rather than inside the quotation marks

Format

"Quoted sentence" (Complete note citation).

Example

"An up-close look at the pilier columns and vault ribs reveals that the magnificent concave and convex shapes of the cathedral were created through the relatively low-tech methods of printing and stamping, similar to how Jell-o retains the shape of a mold" (Victor Wishna, "A New Look at Old Buildings," Humanities, Mar. 2005, http://www.neh.gov/news/humanities/2005-03/anewlook.html [accessed May 25, 2005]).

Complete citation following block quotation

Insert the full publication information parenthetically after a block quotation. Note that there is a period at the end of the block quotation and there is not a period after the citation or the closing parentheses.

Format

Block quotation. (Full publication information)

Example

Outside North America's boardrooms, farmers were in an economic depression. Wheat prices bottomed out at a quarter of what they were right after the Civil War, falling from $2.06 a bushel in 1866 to just 49 cents in 1894. While costs of everything were down, farmers' long-term acquisitions—farmland or machines bought in better times—ate up more of their reduced income. (Randy Leffingwell, *Farm Tractors* [Hong Kong: Lowe & B. Hould, 2002], 9)

Poetry block quotation

With poetry citations, place the parenthetical citation on a separate line from the quotation. Section 11.83 in the *Chicago Manual of Style* suggests centering the citation on the longest line in the quotation and indicating line or stanza numbers as needed.

Format

Block quotation.

    (citation)

Example

Men say they know many things;

But lo! they have taken wings—

The arts and sciences,

And a thousand appliances;

The wind that blows

Is all that any body knows.

    (Thoreau, "Men Say They Know Many Things")

Notes

Notes can be used to provide your reader with bibliographic information or comments regarding information in your text. If you are unsure which type of note to use, consult the following section.

Use footnotes if...

- The reader will benefit from the immediacy of being able to read a note that appears on the same page as its corresponding text

- Notes will enhance the reader's understanding of particular information in the text

- Notes are relatively short and sparse—their presence in the footer of the text body page will not detract from the reader's ability to understand the main text

Use endnotes if...

- Notes require special character effects or figures that could distract readers from your main text, such as tables, etc.

- Only a portion of the intended audience will find the note helpful or interesting

Footnotes

Use footnotes in addition to your bibliography to indicate source publication information for specific parts of your text. Footnotes make it convenient for your readers to check a source without losing their focus as they read. After you have cited material in your text, direct your readers to the appropriate footnote with a superscripted number. The superscript number corresponds to the footnote with the same number at the bottom of the page. Some notes provide supplementary information. See *Notes: Special Circumstances* on page 157 for further details.

First note reference

Provide complete publication information.

Format

Note #. Author full name, *Source title* (Publication city, Publication state: Publisher name, Unabbreviated year published), Page numbers.

Example

3. Peggy Pie, *The Historian's Cookbook* (New York: Practical Press, 31 December 1989), 312.

Subsequent note references

Provide enough information for the reader to find the source's publication information in the bibliography or first note reference.

Format

Note #. Author last name, Page numbers.

Example

3. Pie, 312.

Endnotes

Endnotes provide complete publication information for cited material or supplementary information. Put a superscript after the information in the text that needs a note.

Numbering

The endnote number refers to a specific part of the text body.

Placement

Endnotes appear on their own page at the end of the text.

Page layout

In addition to following the guidelines below, you might also see *Figure 6.4.*

Indentation

Indent the first line of each note with 3 to 5 spaces.

Number Format

Type the superscript number in the text as the endnote number, but not in superscript form. Put a period and a space after the endnote number.

Spacing

Double-space throughout the notes page.

Format

Endnote #. Author full name, *Source title* (Publication city, Publication state: Publisher name, Unabbreviated year published), Page numbers.

3. Peggy Pie, *The Kooky Cook's Cookie Cookbook* (New York: Sweet Tooth Press, 31 December 1989), 312.

Notes: Special Circumstances

This section explains exceptions to standard note formats.

Unnumbered notes

Classical and translated literature

Use unnumbered notes with classical and translated literature.

Purpose

Unnumbered footnotes can provide supplementary information to the text while omitting citations and superscripts that typically interrupt text body content.

Placement

Use unnumbered notes in the footer before any numbered footnotes.

Components

1. The noted section's line number (when already indicated in the text) and/or the page number where the endnote number would normally appear

2. A keyword relating to the text

3. Your note about the keyword

Format variations

The keyword can be italicized or bracketed.

Line # and/or Page # *keyword* Note information

Or

Line # and/or Page # [keyword] Note information

Example

In this example, 13 is the page number where poverty (the keyword) is mentioned in the text. "Assuming the poverty level stays constant" is the note information that the author wanted to tell the reader, but it was not an imperative part of the text.

13   *poverty*   Assuming the poverty level stays constant

14   *population*   Atypical decrease as is evident from fig. 12

21   *two hundred*   This is an estimate from 27 studies conducted over a four year period across Chichester and Wyndoc Counties

Reprinted publications

Purpose

Use an unnumbered footnote to indicate the source of reprinted material, such as in an anthology.

Placement

Place the footnote on the first page of text, before any numbered footnotes.

Format variations

The format differs depending on whether the reprinted material's title is the same as its original title.

When a reprinted document title is the same as the original title, use this format:

Format

Reprinted with permission from copyright holder name, *Publication title* (Publication city: Publisher, Year published), Page number starts-Ends.

Example

Reprinted with permission from Lehan Patterson, *Family Structures* (San Diego: BeeLine, 2005), 76-90.

When a reprinted document title differs from the original title, use this format:

•

Format

Originally published as "Original document title," *Original publication title*, Volume or issue # (Year published): Page number starts-Ends, © Copyright year by Copyright holder name. All Rights Reserved. Reprinted by permission.

Example

Originally published as "Cultural Implications of Theft," *Legal Enforcement*, no. 1 (2001): 2-40, © 2001 by Frenwin Community College. All Rights Reserved. Reprinted by permission.

Honorable acknowledgement

Purpose

Use unnumbered notes to acknowledge an author or contributor when you do not want to interrupt the text with superscripts or when the note is not relevant to the text.

Placement

Use unnumbered notes in the footer before any numbered footnotes. Format the note as a footnote regardless of whether your work only uses endnotes.

Format

A footnote without a number

Example

SourceAid extends its appreciation to Ted Phillips and Nathan Johnson for their generous support.

Volumes

One of multiple volumes published in one year
Indicate the volume number with a colon followed by page numbers.

> **Format**
>
> Note #. Author full name, *Source title* (Publication city, Publication state: Publisher name, Unabbreviated year published), Volume #: Page numbers.

The only volume published during the source's publication year

Indicate the volume number with the abbreviation `vol.` within the note.

> **Format**
>
> Note #. Author full name, *Source title*, vol. Volume number, *Volume title* (Publication city, Publication state: Publisher name, Unabbreviated year published), Page numbers.

Dates

If you have several notes containing dates, you can increase readability by using the Day Month Year format, rather than the traditional Month Day, Year arrangement.

Understanding CMS Terminology

Be aware that there are certain indicator words that must be included in your citations to further describe a source being cited to your reader. These indicators clarify the source's media form and explain the roles of the people included in the citation. Keep an eye out for these indicators when working with the citation formats in the following section.

People indicators

Your reader must be able to immediately recognize the roles of people included in your citations. Without certain indicators, it would be hard for a reader to distinguish a person's role.

Table 6.1

Role Designators of People in Citations

Common Indicators	Meaning
Editor	Editor
ed. or eds.	Editor or editors
Translated by	Precedes translator name
trans.	Translator
Compiler	Compiler
comp. or comps.	Compiler(s)

Media type indicators

Table 6.2

Descriptions for Cited Media Types

Media Type Indicators	Meaning
CD-ROM	CD-ROM for computer software
DVD-ROM	DVD-ROM for computer software
Audiocassette	Audiocassette for sound recordings
CD	CD for sound recordings
DVD	Film or program on DVD
Videocassette	Film or program on videocassette

Common terms

To represent your sources accurately, include explanatory indicators where necessary in citations.

Table 6.3

Common Explanatory Terms

Explanatory Indicators	Meaning
Vol. or vol.	Precedes volume number
Review of	Precedes review titles
art.	Article
amend.	Amendment
sec.	Section
cl.	Clause
email message to	Precedes email title
Rep.	Precedes report identification number
Interview with	Precedes interviewee name
no.	Precedes issue number
fol.	Precedes folio information
File	Precedes file information
Accessed	Precedes internet retrieval date
pers. comm.	Personal communication
diss.	Dissertation
site now discontinued	Follows URL of discontinued website

Citation Formats

For additional help adjusting CMS note citations refer to *Notes: Special Circumstances* on page 157.

0. Multiple Authors and Editors

The formats below show how to cite sources with multiple editors and authors but keep in mind these two rules:

1. Cite no more than ten authors in an entry.

2. If there are eleven or more authors, list only the first seven followed by `, et al.`.

0a. Multiple Authors

Bibliographic Entry

Author 1 last name, First name Middle initial., Author 2 first name Middle initial. Last name, and Author 3 first name Middle initial. Last name.

Note

Author 1 first name Middle initial. Last name, Author 2 first name Middle initial. Last name, and Author 3 first name Middle initial. Last name.

0b.   Editor(s) with Author(s)

Cite the authors' names first, followed by the source title and the editor(s). In bibliography citations for sources with both editor(s) and author(s), always use the term `Edited by`. In notes, use the abbreviation `ed.`. The abbreviation `eds.` should not appear in the middle of the citation. Omit abbreviations in shortened notes.[2]

The following format is for a source with two or more authors and editors.

Bibliographic Entry

Author last name, First name Middle initial., and Author first name Middle initial. Last name. *Source title.* Edited by Editor first name Middle initial. Last name and Editor first name Middle initial. Last name.

Note

Author first name Middle initial. Last name and Author first name Middle initial. Last name, *Source title*, ed. Editor first name Middle initial. Last name and Editor first name Middle initial. Last name.

0c.   Editor(s) (No Author)

As shown in the subsequent format, for one editor without an author, cite the editor's name followed by , `ed.`. When there is more than one editor, cite their names followed by , `eds.`.

Bibliographic Entry

Editor last name, First name Middle initial., ed.

Note

Editor first name Middle initial. Last name., ed.

Ch. 6

---

[2] The first time that you cite a particular source, it is a complete note citation. Any note references thereafter are shortened.

0d. Translators and Compilers (With Author)

Cite the author's name first, followed by the source's title. Then cite the editors', translators', and/or compilers' names in the order in which they appear on the source's title page.

Translators

In a complete note citation for one or more translators with an author, cite the translator's name followed by , `trans`.. In a bibliography entry for one or more translators with an author, cite the translator's name after the phrase `Translated by`.

Compilers (With Author)

In a complete note citation for one or more compilers with an author, cite the compiler's name followed by , `comp`.. In a bibliography entry for one or more compilers with an author, cite the translator's name after the phrase `Compiled by`.

0e. Translators and Compilers (No Author)

Cite a translator's name with the editor's name (if applicable) in the same order as they appear on the source's title page.

For one or more translators without an author, cite the translator's name followed by , `trans`.. For one compiler without an author, cite the compiler's name followed by , `comp`.. For two or more compilers, cite the compiler's name followed by , `comps`..

1.   Book

1a.   Basic Author

Bibliographic Entry

Author last name, First name Middle initial. *Book title.* Edition # ed. *Series title.* Vol. #, *Volume title.* Edited by Editor first name Middle initial. Last name. Publication city: Publisher, Year published.

Example

```
Max, Hastings. The Second World War: A World
    in Flames. Essential History Special. Vol.
    3. Edited by Alexander Stilwell. Oxford:
    Osprey Publishing, 2004.
```

Note

Note #. Author first name Middle initial. Last name, *Book title.* ed. and/or trans. and/or comp. Editor/Translator/Compiler first name Middle initial. Last name (Publication city, Publication state: Publisher, Year published) Page number starts-Ends.

Example

```
    1. Hastings Max, The Second World War: A
World in Flames. ed. Alexander Stilwell
(Oxford, UK: Osprey Publishing, 2004) 3-4.
```

1b.   Group Author

Bibliographic Entry

Association, company, or committee. *Book title.* Edition # ed. *Series title.* Vol. # of *Volume title.* Edited by Editor first name Middle initial. Last name. Publication city: Publisher, Year published.

Note

Note #. Association, company, or committee, *Book title.* ed. and/or trans. and/or comp. Editor/Translator/Compiler first name Middle initial. Last name (Publication city, Publication state: Publisher, Year published) Page number starts-Ends.

Ch. 6

1c. Chapter or Section

When citing a section with a standard title (such as introduction, preface, or afterwards), insert that term as a section title before the book title.

Bibliographic Entry

Author last name, First name Middle initial. "Chapter/section title," *Book title*. Edition # ed. *Series title*. Vol. #, *Volume title*. Edited by Editor first name Middle initial. Last name. Publication city: Publisher, Year published.

Example

```
Max, Hastings. "The Second World War: A World
    in Flames," Essential History Special. Vol.
    3. Edited by Alexander Stilwell. Oxford:
    Osprey Publishing, 2004.
```

Note

Note #. Author first name Middle initial. Last name, "Chapter or section title," *Book title*. ed. and/or trans. and/or comp. Editor/Translator/Compiler first name Middle initial. Last name (Publication city, Publication state: Publisher, Year published) Page number starts-Ends.

Example

```
    1. Hastings Max, The Second World War: A
World in Flames. ed. Alexander Stilwell
(Oxford, UK: Osprey Publishing, 2004) 3-4.
```

1d.   CD-ROM

Bibliographic Entry

Author last name, First name Middle initial. *Book title.* Edition # ed. Vol. Volume #, *Volume title.* Edited by Editor first name Middle initial. Last name. Publication city, Publication state: Publisher, Year published. CD-ROM.

Note

Note #. Author first name Middle initial. Last name, *Book title.* ed. and/or trans. and/or comp. Editor/Translator/Compiler first name Middle initial. Last name (Publication city, Publication state: Publisher, Year published), CD-ROM

1e.   Online

Bibliographic Entry

Author last name, First name Middle initial. *Book title.* Ordinal Edition ed. Vol. Volume #, *Volume title.* Edited by Editor first name Middle initial Last name. Publication city, Publication state: Publisher, Year published. URL (accessed Date accessed month Day, Year).

Note

Note #. Author first name Middle initial. Last name, *Book title.* ed. and/or trans. and/or comp. Editor/Translator/Compiler first name Middle initial. Last name (Publication city, Publication state: Publisher, Year published) Page number starts-Ends, URL (accessed Date accessed month Day, Year).

Ch. 6

2. Blog

2a. Entry

Note

Note #. Author first name Middle initial. Last name, "Entry title," Blog title, Organization name, Entry posted month Day, Year. URL (accessed Date accessed month Day, Year).

2b. Comment

Note

Note #. Commenter first name Middle initial. Last name, comment on "Entry title," Blog title, Organization name, Comment posted month Day, Year. URL (accessed Date accessed month Day, Year).

3. Classical, Medieval, and Early English Literary

3a. General

Bibliographic Entry

Author last name, First name Middle initial., Edited by Editor first name Middle initial. Last name Volume # vol. Publication city, Publication state: Publisher, Year published.

Note

Note #. Author first name Middle initial. Last name, Section number.

3b. Classical Works

In note citations, do not use punctuation between the author and the title, or between the title and section number.

4.   E-mail

Bibliographic Entry

E-mail messages to authors appear in the text or in notes. Try to exclude personal e-mail messages from bibliographies. If you must include one in a bibliography, get the author's permission first.

Note

Note #. Author first name Middle initial. Last name, e-mail message to the author, Month Day, Year.

Example

```
     4. John Barb, e-mail message to the author,
Feb. 4, 2005.
```

5.   Encyclopedia or Dictionary

5a.   General

Bibliographic Entry

Encyclopedia or dictionary citations are usually not included in CMS bibliographies.

Note

Note #. *Encyclopedia or dictionary title*, Edition number ed., s.v. "Keyword."

Example

```
     5. The Encyclopedia of World History, 6
ed., s.v. "Civil War."
```

5b.   Online

Bibliographic Entry

Encyclopedia or dictionary citations are usually not included in CMS bibliographies.

Note

Online Encyclopedia or Dictionary Title, edition # ed., s.v. "Keyword," URL (accessed Month Day, Year).

6. Film or Videotape

Bibliographic Entry

"Chapter title." *Film or videotape title*. VHS or DVD. Directed by Director first name Middle initial Last name. Produced by Producer first name Middle initial. Last name. Production city, State: Producer, Year produced.

Note

Note #. "Chapter title," *Film or videotape title*, VHS or DVD, directed by Director first name Middle initial. Last name (Production city, Production state: Producer, Year produced).

7. Government Document

Bibliographic Entry

Government department. Executive or legislative group name. Contributing body. *Document title*. By Author first name Middle initial. Last name. Document #. Year created. Publication city, Year published. S. for Senate or H. for House Rep. Report ID.

Example

U.S. Congress. House. Department of Homeland Security. *Department of Homeland Security Authorization Act for Fiscal Year 2006*. By Christopher Cox. Doc. f:hr071p1.109. 2005. N.p., n.d. H. Rep. 109-71.

Note

Note #. Government department, Executive or legislative group name, Contributing body, *Document title*, Congress # Cong., Session # sess., S. for Senate or H. for House Rep. Report ID, Page number starts-Ends.

Example

7. U.S. Congress, House, Department of Homeland Security, *Department of Homeland Security Authorization Act for Fiscal Year 2006*, 109th Cong., 1st sess., H 109-71.

8. Interview

Published interview citations vary depending on whether you cite them directly or indirectly in your text.

8a. Directly Quoted

Bibliographic Entry

Interviewer last name, First name Middle initial. "Interview title." Interview with Interviewee first name Middle initial. Last name. In *Publication or production title*, ed. Editor first name Middle initial. Last name. *Edition title* (Publication city: Publisher, Interview date month Day, Year), Page number cited starts-Ends.

Noto

Interviewer first name Middle initial. Last name, "Interview title" (interview with Interviewee first name Middle initial. Last name, in *Publication or production title*, ed. Editor first name Middle initial. Last name, *Edition title* (Publication city: Publisher, Interview date month Day, Year), Page number starts-Ends.

8b. Indirectly Quoted

Bibliographic Entry

Interviewee last name, First name Middle initial. "Interview title." By Interviewer first name Middle initial. Last name. Publisher (Interview date month Day, Year): Page number starts-Ends.

Note

Note #. Interviewee first name Middle initial. Last name, interview by Interviewer first name Middle initial. Last name, "Interview title," Publisher, Interview date month Day, Year.

8c. Unpublished

Bibliographic Entry

CMS recommends citing unpublished interviews as notes.

Note

Interviewee first name Middle initial. Last name, interview by Interviewer first name Middle Initial. Last name, Interview date month Day, Year, Interview description, Interview location facility name, City, State.

Example

8. Ashley T. Parisini, interview by Antonio Tuscano, July 15, 1980, A Roman Tale, Centerville Public Library, Centerville, MA.

9. Journal Article

Unless spelling out abbreviated names is helpful to the reader, present the authors' names as they appear in the journal article's heading,

Publication date tips:

- Include volume number, issue number, or year.

- Whenever possible, include a season, a month, or an exact day.

9a. General

Bibliographic Entry

Author last name, First name Middle initial. "Article title: Article subtitle." *Periodical title* Volume #, no. Issue # (Year published): Page number starts-Ends.

Example

Bradley, Curtis A. and Jack L. Goldsmith. "Congressional authorization and the war on terrorism." *Harvard Law Review* 118, no. 7 (2005): 2047-2133.

Ch. 6

Note

Note #. Author first name Middle initial. Last name, "Article title," *Periodical title* Volume #, no. Issue # (Year published): Page number starts-Ends.

Example

```
     9. Curtis A. Bradley and Jack L. Goldsmith,
"Congressional authorization and the war on
terrorism," Harvard Law Review 118, no. 7
(2005): 2047-2133.
```

9b.   Online

Bibliographic Entry

Author last name, First name Middle initial. "Article title." *Periodical title* Volume #, no. Issue # (Year published): Page number starts-Ends. URL (accessed Date accessed month Day, Year).

Note

Note #. Author first name Middle initial. Last name, "Article title," *Periodical title* Volume #, no. Issue # (Year published), Page number starts-Ends, URL (accessed Date accessed month Day, Year).

10.   Lecture or Meeting Presentation

Bibliographic Entry

Speaker last name, First name Middle initial. "Paper or lecture title." Lecture or presentation type, Host organization, City, State, Lecture or presentation month Day, Year.

Example

```
Foner, Eric. "The Idea of Freedom in the
     American Century." Lecture, East Carolina
     University, Greenville, NC, November 2002.
```

Note

Note #. Speaker first name Middle initial. Last name, "Paper or lecture title," (Lecture or presentation type, Host organization, City, State, Lecture or presentation month Day, Year).

Example

> 10. Eric Foner, "The Idea of Freedom in the American Century," (lecture, East Carolina University, Greenville, NC, November 2002).

11. Legal Cases

11a. U.S. Supreme Court Report Decision (Published)

Note

Note #. *Case or court decision title*, Volume # U.S. Ordinal series # (Decision year).

Example

> 11. *Brown v. Board of Education*, 374 U.S. 483 (1954).

11b. U.S. Supreme Court Decision (Not Published in U.S. Supreme Court Report)

Note

Note #. *Case or court decision title*, Volume # S. Ct. Ordinal series # (Decision year).

11c. Lower Federal Courts

Note

Note #. *Case or court decision title*, Volume # F./F.Supp. Ordinal series # (Deciding court name Decision year).

11d. Subsequent Note to Whole Decision

Note

Note #. *First non-governmental party name*, Volume # Reporter series name Ordinal series #.

11e.   Subsequent Note to Page in Same Source

Note

Note #. *First non-governmental party name*, Volume # Reporter series name Ordinal series # at page number cited.

12.   Letter in Published Collection

Bibliographic Entry

Author last name, First name Middle initial. Letter to Recipient first name Middle initial. Last name. Date created day Month Year. *Collection Title*, Edited by Editor first name Middle initial. Last name, [fol.Folio # or fols.Folio # starts-Ends or Page number starts-Ends]. Publication city: Publisher, Year published.

Example

```
Spangler, Paul E. Letter to Friend. Dec. 7,
    1941. War Letters: Extraordinary
    Correspondence from American Wars, Edited
    by Andrew Carroll, [184-186]. New York:
    2001.
```

Note

Note #. Author first name Middle initial. Last name to Recipient first name Middle initial. Last name, Date created day Month Year, file File ID, *Collection title*, Depository or institution name, City.

Example

```
    12. Paul E. Spangler to Friend, 7 Dec.
1941, War Letters: Correspondence from
American Wars.
```

13. Magazine Article

If the article title is a headline, then capitalize it as you would a sentence.

Example

Professors rage over dropping salaries.

If the article title is formal, then capitalize the important words.

Example

The Death Penalty Debate

Cite magazine articles by date and exclude volume and issue numbers.

Cite specific page numbers in notes. Use a comma (as opposed to a colon) to separate it from the publication date.

13a. Author, but not Department, is Known

Bibliographic Entry

Author last name, First name Middle initial. "Article title." *Periodical title*, Date published month Day, Year, Page number starts-Ends.

Example

```
McCullough, David. "History: 1776--
    Washington's War; Prone to doubt, George
    Washington never lost faith. Behind his
    mask of command." Newsweek, May 23, 2005,
    42.
```

Note

Note #. Author first name Middle initial. Last name, "Article title," *Periodical title*, Date published month Day, Year, Page number starts-Ends.

Example

13. David McCullough, "History: 1776—Washington's War; Prone to doubt, George Washington never lost faith. Behind the mask of command," *Newsweek*, May 23, 2005, 42.

13b.   Author and Department are Known

Bibliographic Entry

Author last name, First name Middle initial. Department, "Article title." *Periodical title*, Date published month Day, Year, Page number starts-Ends.

Note

Note #. Author first name Middle initial. Last name, Department, "Article title," *Periodical title*, Date published day Month Year, Page number starts-Ends.

13c.   Department, but not Author, is Known

Bibliographic Entry

Periodical title. Department. "Article title." Date published month Day, Year, Page number starts-Ends.

Note

Note #. *Periodical title*, Department, "Article title," Date published day Month Year, Page number starts-Ends.

13d.   Author, but not Department, is Known (Online)

Bibliographic Entry

Author last name, First name Middle initial. "Article title." *Periodical title*, Date published month Day, Year, URL (accessed Date accessed month Day, Year).

Ch. 6

Note

Note #. Author first name Middle initial. Last name, "Article title," *Periodical title*, Date published day Month Year, Page number starts-Ends.

13e.   Author and Department are Known (Online)

Bibliographic Entry

Author last name, First name Middle initial. Department, "Article title." *Periodical title*, Date published month Day, Year, URL (accessed Date accessed month Day, Year).

Note

Note #. Author first name Middle initial. Last name, Department, "Article title," *Periodical title*, Date published day Month Year, URL (accessed Date accessed month Day, Year).

13f.   Department, but not Author, is Known (Online)

Bibliographic Entry

Periodical title. Department. "Article title." Date published month Day, Year. URL (accessed Date accessed month Day, Year).

Note

Note #. *Periodical title*, Department, "Article title," Date published day Month Year, URL (accessed Date accessed month Day, Year).

14.   Manuscript Collections

Bibliographic Entry

Author last name, First name Middle initial., Document title. Collection name. Depository name, City, State.

Note

Note #. Document title, Item date, Author first name Middle initial. Last name, Depository name, City, State.

15. Microform

Cite microform sources as you would a book, but indicate the form (fiche, microfilm, and so forth) after the publication facts. In a note, specify the relative location, such as p. 102, 4P38, if possible.

16. Newspaper Article

CMS recommends citing a newspaper article in a note instead of in your bibliography.

16a. General

Bibliographic Entry

Author last name, First name Middle initial. "Article title." *Periodical title*, Date published month Day, Year, Edition description, sec. Section #.

Example

Wright, Robert. "Terror in the Past and Future Tense." *The New York Times*, April 26, 2005, sec. A.

Note

Note #. Author first name Middle initial. Last name "Article title," *Periodical title*, sec. Section #, Date published month Day, Year.

Example

16. Robert Wright, "Terror in Past and Future Tense," *The New York Times*, sec. A, April 26, 2005.

16b. Online

Bibliographic Entry

Author last name, First name Middle initial. "Article title." *Periodical title*, Date published month Day, Year, sec. Section number. URL (accessed Date accessed month Day, Year).

Note

Note #. Author first name Middle initial. Last name ,"Article title," *Periodical title*, sec. Section number, Date published month Day, Year, URL (accessed Date accessed month Day, Year).

17. Online Database

Use the citation format (news, journal, or scientific database) that applies to your source.

17a. News or Journal

Bibliographic Entry

Author last name, First name Middle initial. "Document title." *Periodical title* Volume #, no. Issue # (Year published): Page number starts-Ends. Database main entrance URL ending in a slash (accessed Date accessed month Day, Year).

Example

```
Lorenz, Alfred L. "Ralph W. Tyler: The unknown
     correspondent of World War I." Journalism
     History 31, no.1 (2005): http://
     www.infotrac.com/ (accessed June 5, 2005).
```

Note

Note #. Author first name Middle initial. Last name, "Document title," *Periodical title*, Publication month Day, Year, Edition number in letters edition, Database main entrance URL ending in a slash (accessed Date accessed month Day, Year).

Example

```
     17. Alfred L. Lorenz, "Ralph W. Tyler: The
unknown correspondent of World War I,"
Journalism History, 2005, http://
www.infotrac.com/ (accessed June 5, 2005).
```

17b.   Scientific

Bibliographic Entry

Database name. Main URL ending in a slash (Part of database cited or descriptive phrase; accessed month Day, Year).

Note

Note #. Database name, Main URL ending in a slash (Part of database cited or descriptive phrase; accessed month Day, Year).

18.   Online Posting

Bibliographic Entry

Author last name, First name Middle initial. "String title." Date created month Day, Year. URL (accessed Date accessed month Day, Year).

Example
```
Yun, "Mongols capture emperor." Mar. 18, 2005.
    http://www.chinahistoryforum.com/
    index.php?showtopic=2988 (accessed June 5,
    2005).
```

Note

Note #. Author first name Middle initial. Last name, "String title," Date created month Day, Year, URL (accessed Month Day, Year).

Example
```
    18. Yun, "Mongols capture emperor," Mar.
18, 2005, http://www.chinahistoryforum.com/
index.php?showtopic=2988 (accessed June 5,
2005).
```

Ch. 6

19.   Pamphlet or company report

Cite pamphlets, corporate reports, brochures, and similar publications as you would a book. If you are missing any information, such as author and publisher, give enough supplementary information to help the reader identify the document.

20.   Personal Communication

Bibliographic Entry

Personal Communication sources are cited in notes and text citations, but are usually not included in the bibliography.

Note

Note #. First name Middle initial. Last name, pers. comm., Date communicated month Day, Year.

Example

```
    20. James H. Miller, pers. comm., Sept. 16,
2004.
```

21.   Podcast

Podcasts are cited in notes and text citations, but are usually not included in the bibliography.

Note

Note #. Producer first name Middle initial. Last name, Podcast title, Publication country: Distributor, Publication month Day, Year, URL (accessed Date accessed month Day, Year).

22.   Real-Time Communication

Bibliographic Entry

Communication group name. Date created month Day, Year. Group Discussion. URL (accessed Date accessed month Day, Year).

Example

```
Civil War Buffs. Nov. 12, 2001. Group
    Discussion. www.chathistory.org. (accessed
    Dec. 14, 2001).
```

Note

Note #. Communication group name, Date created month Day, Year, Group Discussion, URL (accessed Date accessed Day Month Year)

Example

```
    22. Civil War Buffs, November 12, 2001,
Group Discussion, www.chathistory.org
(accessed 14 December 2001).
```

23.   Review

23a.   Book Review

Bibliographic Entry

Reviewer last name, First name Middle initial. "Review title." Review of *Book Reviewed* by Reviewed source author first name Middle initial. Last name. *Publication title* (Date published month Day, Year): Page number starts-Ends.

Example

```
Pearce, Robert. "Chronological History of US
    Foreign Relations." Review of Chronological
    History of US Foreign Relations, by Lester
    H. Brune and Richard D. Burns. History
    Review 49 (Sept. 2004): 56.
```

Note

Note #. Reviewer first name Middle initial Last name, Review of *Book Reviewed*, by Reviewed source author first name Middle initial. Last name, ed./trans. Editor/Translator first name Middle initial. Last name, *Publication title* (Date published month Day, Year): Page number starts-Ends.

Example

```
     23. Robert Pearce, Review of Chronological
History of US Foreign Relations, by Lester H.
Brune and Richard D. Burns, History Review 49
(Sept. 2004): 56.
```

23b. Film or Play Review

Bibliographic Entry

Reviewer last name, First name Middle initial. "Review title." Review of *Film/Play Reviewed*, directed by Director first name Middle initial. Last name, Theater or location performed. *Publication title*, Date published month Day, Year, Periodical section.

Note

Note #. Reviewer first name Middle initial. Last name, review of *Film/Play Reviewed*, directed by Director first name Middle initial. Last name, Theater or location performed, *Publication title,* Date published month Day, Year, Periodical section.

24.   Sacred Text

24a.   Single Verse

Bibliographic Entry

Sacred texts are usually cited in notes instead of bibliographies.

Note

Note #. Abbreviated book title Chapter #: Verse starts-Ends (Version name).

Example

    24. Matt 5:1-14 (New American Standard Bible).

24b.   Multiple Verses

Bibliographic Entry

It is usually best to cite sacred texts in notes instead of bibliographies.

Note

Note #. Abbreviated book title Chapter #: Verse starts-Ends, Chapter #: Verse starts-Ends.

25.   Sound Recording

Sound recordings are often given their own section and subheading in bibliographies.

Bibliography Entry

Composer last name, First name Middle initial. *Work title.* Producing agency. Recorder or conductor first name Middle initial Last name. Media type (i.e. Audiocassette, Compact disc, etc.).

Example

    Roosevelt, Franklin D. *Fireside chat on the Reorganization of the Judicial Branch of the United States Government.* CBS. Radio.

Note

Note #. Composer or performer first name Middle initial. Last name, *Work title*, Producing agency, Recorder or conductor first name Middle initial. Last name, Media type (i.e. Audiocassette, Compact disc, etc.).

Example

    25. Franklin D. Roosevelt, *Fireside Chat on
    the Reorganization of the Judicial Branch of
    the United States Government*, CBS, Radio.

26.   Source Quoted in Other Source

Citing a source that you have not examined is not recommended. If the original source is unattainable, and you must cite a source quoted in one of your sources, then include both sources in the citation.

Bibliographic Entry

Author last name, First name Middle initial. *Quoted work title*, Page number starts-Ends. Publication city, State: Publisher, Publication month Year published. Quoted in Author first name Middle initial Last name, *Source title* (Publication city, State: Publisher, Year published), Page number starts-Ends.

Example

Gatewood, Willard. *Smoked Yankees and the
    Struggle for Empire*, 310. Fayetteville, AR:
    University of Arkansas Press, 1987. Quoted
    in Howard Zinn, *A People's History of the
    Unites States* (New York: Harper Collins,
    1995), 310.

Note

Note #. Author first name Middle initial. Last name,"Quoted work title," (Publication month Year): Page number starts-Ends, quoted in Author first name Middle initial. Last name, *Source Title* (Publication city, State: Publisher, Year published), Page number starts-Ends.

Example

```
26. Willard Gatewood, "Smoked Yankees and
the Struggle for Empire," (1987): 310, quoted
in Howard A. Zinn, A People's History of the
United States (New York, NY: Harper Collins
1995), 310.
```

27.   Unpublished Dissertation or Thesis

Bibliographic Entry

Speaker last name, First name Middle initial. "Dissertation title." Thesis type, diss., Host organization, Presentation month Day, Year.

Example

```
Barlow, J. A. "A Constraint-based Account of
    Syllable Onsets: Evidence from developing
    systems." Master's thesis diss., Indiana
    University, 1997.
```

Note

Note #. Speaker first name Middle initial. Last name, "Dissertation title," (Thesis type diss., Host organization, Presentation month Day, Year).

Example

```
27. J. A. Barlow, "A Constraint-based
Account of Syllable Onsets: Evidence from
developing systems," (master's thesis diss.,
Indiana University, 1997).
```

Ch. 6

28. Web Site

Web sites are best cited in notes, but may be cited as bibliographic citations in compositions without notes. When the content's author is unknown, the web site owner replaces the author as the first and foremost component of a citation.

28a. Entire Web Site

Bibliographic Entry

Content author last name, First name Middle initial. Site owner or *title*. URL (accessed Date accessed month Day, Year).

Example

```
Henige, Chris. History of Art.
    http://www.beloit.edu/~arthist/
    historyofart/index.htm (accessed June 11,
    2005).
```

Note

Note #. Content author first name Middle Initial. Last name, Site owner or *title*, URL (accessed Date accessed month Day, Year).

Example

```
    28. Chris Henige, History of Art,
http://www.beloit.edu/~arthist/historyofart/
index.htm (accessed June 11, 2005).
```

28b. Discontinued Web Site

Bibliographic Entry

Content author last name, First name Middle initial. Site owner or *title*. Organization name. URL (accessed Date accessed month Day, Year; site now discontinued).

Note

Note #. Content author first name Middle initial. Last name, Site owner or *title* URL (accessed Date accessed month Day, Year; site now discontinued).

28c. Web Document (Author Known)

Bibliographic Entry

Author last name, First name Middle initial. "Article title." *Site title*. Organization name. URL (accessed Date accessed month Day, Year).

Example

```
Topulos, Katherine. "General Legal Research
     Sites." Internet Research. Duke Law.
     http://www.law.duke.edu/lib/researchguides/
     intresearch.html#gen (accessed June 3,
     2005).
```

Note

Note #. Author first name Middle initial. Last name, "Article Title," *Site title*, Organization name, URL (accessed Date accessed month Day, Year).

Example

```
     28. Katherine Topulos, "General Legal
Research Sites," Internet Research, Duke Law,
http://www.law.duke.edu/lib/researchguides/
intresearch.html (accessed June 3, 2005).
```

28d. Web Document (Author Unknown)

Bibliographic Entry

Site owner. "Work title." *Site title*. Organization name. URL (accessed Date accessed month Day, Year).

Note

Note #. Site owner, "Work title," *Site title*, Organization name, URL (accessed Date accessed month Day, Year).

28e. Personal or Informal Web Site

Bibliographic Entry

Site title. Site description. URL (accessed Date accessed month Day, Year).

Note

Note #. *Site title,* Site description, URL (accessed Date accessed month Day, Year).

29. Work in Series

Bibliographic Entry

Author last name, First name Middle initial. *Work title.* Series title #. Publication city: Publisher, Year published.

Example

Field, Ron. *The Confederate Army 1861-65: South Carolina & Mississippi.* Men-at-Arms 1. Oxford, UK: Osprey Publishing, 2005.

Note

Note #. Author first name Middle initial. Last name, *Work title,* Series title # (if any), (Publication city: Publisher, Year published).

Example

29. Ron Field, *The Confederate Army 1861-65: South Carolina & Mississippi,* Men-at-Arms 1, (Oxford, UK: Osprey Publishing, 2005).

Works Cited

Chicago Manual of Style. 15th ed. Chicago: U of Chicago P.
2005.

Leffingwell, Randy. Farm Tractors. Hong Kong: Lowe & B.
Hould, 2002.

Mackenzie, Dana. "Ahead of Its Time?" Smithsonian Mag. Jan.
2005. 25 May 2005
<http://www.smithsonianmag.si.edu/smithsonian/issues05/
jan05/digs.html>.

Thoreau, Henry David. "Men Say They Know Many Things."
Reflections at Walden. Ed. Peter Seymour. Kansas City:
Hallmark Cards, 1968. 53.

Wishna, Victor. "A New Look at Old Buildings." Humanities
Mar. 2005. 25 May 2005 <http://www.neh.gov/news/
humanities.html>.

7 Council of Science Editors

About CSE

What is CSE?

This chapter is consistent with the writing style set forth in *Scientific Style and Format*, 7th Edition, as published by the Council of Science Editors and The Rockefeller University Press. CSE is an abbreviation for the Council of Science Editors and it was previously referred to as CBE, or the Council of Biology Editors.

When should I use CSE?

Use the CSE writing style when researching hard sciences, such as chemistry, biology, and physics.

How is CSE different?

There are three major citation systems that are widely used in CSE, the citation-sequence (C-S) system, the citation-name (C-N) system, and the name-year (N-Y) system. Although the same identifying information is required to cite a source in CSE using any of these three citation systems, each citation system orders this identifying information differently within its corresponding citation formats and reference list.

Citation-Sequence (C-S) System

The citation-sequence system represents in-text citations numerically. The citations in the reference list at the end of your paper are arranged by the order that they appear in your work.

Citation-Name (C-N) System

The citation-name system requires that your reference list be arranged alphabetically by the author's last name. With the reference list arranged alphabetically, the first citation in the reference list is number one, the second citation number two, etcetera. Having compiled and numbered every citation that appears in the reference list, you are then to go back throughout the body of your paper and indicate in-text citations by representing them numerically in the way that corresponds to the numerical reference list. For example, assuming that the first citation in your reference list is a work by Alistair, then that work should be represented numerically as [1] in all in-text citations, regardless of the order in which they appear in your paper's text.

Name-Year (N-Y) System

The name-year system, as its name implies, privileges the author's name and the publication year in parenthetical in-text citations and the alphabetically arranged reference list. Often called the "Harvard system", this way of arranging citations is more like the other writing styles represented in this book.

This manual shows citation formats and examples based on the Name-Year System.

Composition Layout

CSE does not specify requirements for paper formatting and layout. Be sure to talk to your teacher or professor for his or her formatting preferences.

Tables

Location and Arrangement

It is usually appropriate to put CSE tables at the end of your work in the order in which they are mentioned in your paper.

Title

Number each table and label it with a brief explanatory title two spaces after the number.

Example

Table 2 Summary of progesterone levels in pregnant rats

Explanation

Because a table must be self-explanatory, the reader must be able to grasp its meaning without referring to your body text. Further explain any part of a table by footnoting it with a sequential letter superscript and including explanatory information in footnote form on the same page as the table.

Missing information

If your table is missing information because it is unavailable, use the abbreviation ND in an empty cell to indicate that there is "no data".

Figures

Places necessary figures (graphs, maps, charts, photographs, illustrations, etc.) within the body text of your paper immediately following your first mentioning of them.

Reference List

Your complete citation list is called a reference list. Like bibliographies and reference lists in all the other major writing styles, your references must be all-inclusive with accurate and complete citations.

References Layout

Content

Include full publication and identification information for every source cited in the text. You should also include complete citations for each source you reviewed in researching, but did not explicitly reference in your paper. Citations for book and article titles are not underlined or italicized in the CSE format. Aside from proper nouns, proper adjectives, and other accepted capitalized abbreviations, only capitalize the first word in article titles.

Title

Title the page where you will build your reference list `References`.

Spacing

There is no specification in CSE that requires you to double-space citations in your reference list. Again, you should ask your teacher or professor for his or her preference, and create a reference list that is easily readable. Citations can be written in a font size that is smaller than the font used in the paper's body.

Organization

Divide your references into two sections that are clearly marked in the reference list. In the first section, `Cited References`, include the citations for the materials directly cited in your paper. You could also title this section of your reference list `References`, `Literature Cited`, or `Bibliography`. Alphabetize the citations in this first section by the author's last name or the first relevant word of the citation (`A`, `An`, and `The` should be excluded from organization names in the reference list). Create the second section, Additional References, after the Cited References section. Include citation information in alphabetical order for the sources you consulted during research but did not directly include in your paper. This section could also be entitled Additional Reading or Supplemental References.

Ordering and Completing Citations: Special Circumstances

Organization abbreviations

If the author of a work you are citing is an organization with a complex name, CSE recommends that you start your citation in References by including an abbreviation of the organization name in brackets. This bracketed abbreviation precedes the full name of the organization. This abbreviation is what will be used for in-text citations. Do not take the bracketed abbreviation into consideration while alphabetizing your reference list—the organization's full name should determine its alphabetical placement.

Example

[ASCCR] American Society for Clinical Cancer Research. 1998.

Common organization name

If an organization name that is included in your reference is common, specify which organization you are referring to by including the organization's location in parentheses.

Example

American Red Cross (New York).

National organization name

If you are citing a government or national organization whose country of origin is not specified in the organization's title, include the appropriate abbreviation for the country after the organization's name in parentheses.

Example

National Academy of the Arts and Sciences (US)

The Royal Society (GB)

Problematic alphabetization

If the author's last name includes de, la, van, von, etc., treat these as part of the surname and alphabetize them accordingly. Spaces or apostrophes within an author's last name are ignored when alphabetizing, thus the prefixes M', Mc, and Mac should be arranged according to their actual lettering; you should not assume that M', Mc, and Mac all *mean* Mac. McDonough should come before M'Grady. MacGregor comes before McGrath.

Author with numerous publications

If you are referencing many works by the same author in your paper, your reference list should order the citations by the year in which they were published.

Example

Schmitt WE. 2002.

Schmitt WE. 2005.

Author with numerous publications from the same year

If an author published many materials in the same year, list them according to the order of their publication (earliest to latest), and add an alphabetic designator to the citations (a, b, c, etc.) after the year.

Note: You will use this alphabetic designator in your in-text parenthetical citations.

Example

Schmitt WE. 2002a. Genetic diversity in white mice.

Schmitt WE. 2002b. Genetic uniformity in white mice.

Multiple authors

If you are referencing a work that has up to ten authors, include the last name and first initials of every author. If the work you are referencing has more than ten authors, list the first ten authors and conclude the author portion of the citation with `and others`.

A work with ten or less authors

Example

Hagemann RC, McDonough ME, McGrath CK, Merrill MS, Oranburg SC, Patton MB, Rush RJ, Spurlock PE, Toth MR, Van Voorhis EC. 2002.

A work with ten or more authors

Example

Hagemann RC, McDonough ME, McGrath CK, Merrill MS, Oranburg SC, Patton MB, Rush RJ, Spurlock PE, Toth MR, Van Voorhis EC, and others. 2002.

Anonymous author

If the source does not give the author, begin the citation with the next available information in the citation format, the work's title. Do not cite the author as "Anonymous". Do the same with in-text citations. When creating an in-text citation for a pamphlet entitled, "Medical Breakthroughs in the Treatment of Alzheimer's Patients", for example, use the first identifying word(s) of the title followed by an ellipsis as in (Medical breakthroughs...2004).

Forthcoming work

When the work you are citing is not yet printed, but in the process of being printed, you may include it in your reference list and write Forthcoming at the end of your citation. If you know the expected year of publication, include it after this indicator.

Example

If the work you are citing is scheduled to be printed in 2012, include the year in your citation as "Forthcoming 2012".

In-Text Citations

The N-Y system that we focus on in this book uses in-text citations to immediately alert the reader to the author's name and the year of publication of the work being referenced. These citations appear parenthetically in your paper directly following any reference—they can appear mid-sentence. They must include the author's last name (or organization's full or abbreviated name) and the year of publication. It is crucial that the spelling and publication information of your in-text citations matches up perfectly with the spelling and publication information included in your reference list.

Author not cited within text

When you reference a work without directly quoting from it or mentioning the author within the sentence, include the author's last name and the year the source was published in parentheses immediately after it is referenced in the sentence.

Example

The 11th dimension of string theory is said to be a membrane separating parallel universes (Crafford 1998), an idea that has led many to believe...

Author cited within text

When you refer to the author of your source in the context of an explanatory sentence about that author's work, create your in-text citation by adding the year of the publication in parentheses after the author's name is mentioned.

Example

Crafford (1998) explores the idea that the 11th dimension of string theory is a membrane separating parallel universes.

Forthcoming article

When referencing a work that is in the process of being printed, write forthcoming in place of the year. If you are aware of the expected publication date, include it in your in-text citation after "forthcoming".

Example

When the forthcoming publication date is unknown: (Miceli forthcoming).

When the forthcoming publication date is known. (Miceli forthcoming 2010).

Organization is author

An abbreviation for long organizational names should precede the full name of the organization in your reference list. See *Organization abbreviations* on page 199. For your in-text citations, you may use this abbreviation and the publication year. The example below is an in-text citation for a source by the American Society for Clinical Cancer Research; the organization is abbreviated with the abbreviation ASCCR.

Example

Powerful antioxidants in green tea may serve as a deterrent to cancer (ASCCR 1998).

Author with multiple publications cited simultaneously

When referencing several works of the same author at once, list the author's last name and the publication years in chronological order, separated with commas, in your parenthetical citation.

There are ongoing studies regarding the evolutionary implications of the existence of one queen bee within a hive (Nguyen 1994, 1997, 2001).

Author with multiple works published the same year cited simultaneously

When referencing two or more sources by the same author that were published in the same year, indicate their order by adding alphabetic designators (a, b, c, etc.) to the end of the year to show which was published first.

In his work, Matt Nguyen studied the mating habits of the bees in over one hundred bee hives, publishing his results in a quarterly newsletter (1994a, 1994b, 1994c, 1994d).

Co-authored work

When you are referencing a work that is co-authored, include both of the authors' last names in your citation. Use the word and to indicate that the two people are co-authors.

(Ruzika and Spiegel 2004).

More than three authors

When you are referencing a work that has three or more authors, include the last name of the first author and the phrase and others in your citation.

(Goodyear and others 2005).

Multiple works cited simultaneously

When you reference multiple works at once, separate the authors and their respective years with a semicolon in your in-text citation.

Example

(Cinelli 2001; Duffy 2003; Parrella 2003).

Different authors with same surname

When you are referencing two works and both authors have the same surname, be sure to include the initials of both authors so the reader understands which you are referencing.

Example

(O'Brien DS 2002; O'Brien TW 2001).

Specific section of source

When you insert a quotation into your paper or are referencing a specific page in your source, include a page number in your citation after the year.

Example

(Weatherall 1999, p 36).

Notes

Notes can be used to further explain information that is included in tables, or convey information that is supplemental to the body of the paper.

Understanding CSE Terminology

You must include the following indicator words in your reference list.

Common Source Type Indicators

Table 7.1

Source Type Indicators

Common Indicators	Description
[Video] [Audiocassette] [DVD]	Video, Audiocassette, and DVD indicate the source's media type.
[computer program] [abstract] [letter] Suppl	In certain circumstances, you must specify whether the work is a computer program, abstract, editorial, letter, supplement, or online serial article.
[map type]	When prompted to include the map type in brackets, indicate what type of map you are referencing – a world map, a demographic map, etc.

Example
Author. Database title [Medium designator]. Edition. Publication place: publisher. Beginning date-Ending date. Physical description. Notes.

Physical Descriptions

In addition to the common indicators listed in Table 7.1, some citations call for a Physical description optional identifying words that explain source attributes. Attribute examples include the length of a video or DVD, the number of audiocassettes in an audiocassette series, and the system requirements for a computer program.

Publication Dates

Though most Name-Year citation formats only require you to cite your source's year of publication, some source types that are published more frequently (such as newspapers and magazines) require more extensive descriptions of publication date information, as do singular publications such as patents. Internet citations also require you to include the day, month, and year of the website's last update and date accessed. Be sure to follow the specified publication date guidelines in the citation formats at the end of this chapter.

Missing Publication Date

Because the publication year is a crucial element of identification in the Name-Year system, when the exact date or year of publication is missing, cite the copyright year in place of the publication year, signifying this with a lowercase "c" before the year in all in-text and reference list citations.

Example

(Jebb c2006).

Pagination

If you are citing an entire work, you will usually cite the total number of pages in the work followed by an explanatory lowercase p.

Example

465 p.

If you are only citing part of the work put a lowercase p. followed by the exact page number.

Example

p. 376.

When citing several discontinuous pages from a journal or newspaper article, cite all page numbers and separate them with dashes and commas to show their continuity and discontinuity.

Example

8-11, 13-14, 16.

If page numbers are not available, include the total number of pages of the work that you are citing in square brackets at the end of your citation.

Example

[9 p.]

Citation Formats

Before creating your CSE citations, make sure you have looked over the *Understanding CSE Terminology* section.

0.   Multiple Authors and Editors

To properly format multiple authors and editors, refer to *Ordering and Completing Citations: Special Circumstances* on page 199.

1.   Audio/Video Recording

Reference

Author last name First initial Middle initial, author. Editor last name First initial Middle initial, editor. Year published. Recording title [Medium type Audiocassette, Video, DVD, etc]. Corporate producer, producer. Publication city (State): Publisher. Physical description. Series statement. Available from: Vendor name City, State.

Example

```
James FT, author. Marry-Ellen H, editor. 1999.
    Evolution of man [Audiocassette]. William
    M, producer. New York (NY): Audio Partner
    Publishing. 48mins. Available from: Borders
    New York, NY; Worcester Polytechnic
    Institute.
```

2.   Book

2a.   General

Reference

Author last name First initial Middle initial. Year published. Book title. Publication city (State): Publisher. Total pages p.

Example

```
Alberts B, Johnson A. 2002. Molecular biology
    of the cell. New York (NY): Garland
    Publishing. 456 p.
```

2b.   Translated

Reference

Author last name First initial Middle initial. Book title. Year published. Translator last name First initial Middle initial, translator; Editor last name First initial Middle initial, editor. Publication city (State): Publisher. Total pages p. Translation of: Title name.

Example

```
Gorz A. Capitalism, socialism, ecology. 1994.
    Turner C, translator. New York (NY): Verso.
    147 p.
```

2c.   Edited (Entire Book)

Reference

Editor last name First initial Middle initial, editor. Year published. Book title. Edition # ed. Publication city (State): Publisher. Total pages p.

2d.   Edited (Portion of Book)

Reference

Part author last name First initial Middle initial. Year published. Part title. In: Editor last name First initial Middle initial, editor. Book title. Publication city (State): Publisher. Page number starts-Ends.

Ch. 7

2e.   Internet

Reference

Author last name First initial Middle initial. Year published. Book title [Internet]. Edition. Publication city (State): Publisher; [updated Date updated year Month Day; cited Date cited Year Month Day]. Available from: URL

Example

```
Goldman L, Coussens C. 2007. Environmental
    public health impact of disasters:
    Hurricane Katrina, workshop summary
    [Internet]. Washington (DC): The National
    Academies Press; [updated 2007 Jan 10;
    cited 2007 Jun 3]. Available from:
    http://www.nap.edu/catalog/11840.html#toc
```

3.   Conference Proceedings and Papers

3a.   Proceedings

Reference

Editor last name First initial Middle initial. Year published. Publication title. Conference name; Conference date starts-Ends; Conference city (State). Publication city (State): Publisher. p Page starts-Ends.

3b.   Paper Abstract

Reference

Author last name First initial Middle initial. Year published. Abstract title. [abstract]. In: Editor last name First initial Middle initial. Conference name; Conference date starts-Ends; Conference city. Publication city (State): Publisher. p Page starts-Ends. Abstract nr Number.

Ch. 7

Example

Hunt A, Abraham JL, Crawford JA, DeStefano P, Garback C, LaMoy M, Nasishadham D, Hall G. 2003. Levels of household particulate matter (PM) and environmental tobacco smoke (ETS) in the first year of life in a cohort at risk for asthma. [abstract]. 99th International Conference of the American Thoracic Society; Seattle (WA). New York (NY): American Thoracic Society. Abstract nr A852.

3c.   Presentation Paper (Published)

Reference

Author last name First initial Middle initial. Year published. Paper title. In: Editor last name First initial Middle initial, editor. Publication title and/or Conference title; Conference date starts-Ends; Conference city, State. Publication city (State): Publisher. p Page starts-Ends.

Example

Ward P, Shreeve RS. 2001. The deep-sea copepod fauna of the southern ocean: patterns and processes. Copepoda: Developments in Ecology, Biology, and Systematics; 1999 Jul 25-31; Curitiba, Brazil. Netherlands: Kluwer Academic Publishers. p 37-54.

3d.   Presentation Paper (Unpublished)

Author last name First initial Middle initial. Conference date starts-Ends. Paper title. Paper presented at: Conference title. Conference Descriptor; Conference city, State.

Example

Toubeau J. 2006 Jun 13. Life in the subsurface ocean of Europa. Paper presented at: Astrobiology Workshop 2006: Astrobiology and habitability. Brussels, Belgium.

Ch. 7

4.   Dissertation

You must include the type of publication (dissertation, DPhil thesis, MSc thesis) in your citation in brackets as indicated below.

Reference

Author last name First initial Middle initial. Degree year. Dissertation title [Publication type]. Institution city (State): Institution name. Page number starts-Ends. Available from: Publisher, Publication city, State; Dissertation number.

Example

```
Holden K. 2001. Lower abdomen [dissertation].
    Miami (FL): University of Miami. 46-51.
    Available from: UM Publishing, Miami, FL;
    11301.
```

5.   Internet Database

Reference

Database title [Internet]. Date of database's creation-Termination. Release information. Publication city (State): Publisher. [updated Date Updated Year Month Day; cited Date cited year Month Day]. Available from: URL

Example

```
Biological & Agricultural Index [Internet].
    1983-  . Ipswich (MA): EBSCO Publishing.
    [updated 2007 Feb 3; cited 2007 July 1].
    Available from: http://www.epnet.com/
    thisTopic.php?marketID=6&topicID=40
```

6. Journal Article

6a. General

Reference

Author last name First initial Middle initial. Year published. Article title. Journal name Volume number(Issue number): Page number starts-Ends.

Example

```
LeBlunc R. 2002. Spinal nerve damage. North
     American Anatomy Journal 1(14):19-28.
```

6b. Author is an Organization

Reference

[Organization name abbreviation] Organization name, Group within organization. Year Month Day published. Article title. Journal name Volume number(Issue number): Page number starts-Ends.

Example

```
[WHO} World Health Organization. 2004.
     Appropriate body-mass index for Asian
     populations and its implications for policy
     and intervention strategies. Lancet
     363(9403): 157-163.
```

6c. Anonymous Author

Reference

[Anonymous]. Year published. Article title. Journal name Volume number(Issue number): Page number starts-Ends.

Example

```
[Anonymous]. 1996. Human rights in peace
     negotiations. Human Rights Quarterly 18(2):
     249-258.
```

6d. Internet

Reference

Author last name First initial Middle initial. Year published. Article title. Journal title abbreviation [Internet]. [updated Date updated year Month Day; cited Date cited year Month Day]; Volume number(Issue number): Page number starts-Ends. Available from: URL

Example

```
Jetz W, Wilcove DS, Dobson AP. 2007. Projected
    impacts of climate and land-use change on
    the global diversity of birds. PLoS Biology
    [Internet]. [updated 2007 Jun; cited 2007
    Aug 6]; 5(6): 1211-1219. Available from:
    http://biology.plosjournals.org/perlserv/
    ?request=getdocument&doi=10.1371%2Fjournal.
    pbio.0050157
```

7. Legal Document

When citing a legal document in CSE, you must adhere to the citation format proscribed by A Uniform System of Citation, published by the Harvard Law Review.

8. Magazine Article

Reference

Author last name First initial Middle initial. Year Month Day published. Article title. Magazine name: Page number starts-Ends.

Example

```
Kealish D. 2005 July 1. Cell development.
    Scientific American 21-22.
```

9.   Map

Reference

Area represented. Year published. Map title [Map type].
In: Atlas name. Publication city (State): Publisher.
Physical description.

Example

```
Boston. 2002. Boston, MA [Road]. Maspeth (New
    York): American Map. 2002 Road Atlas.
```

10.   Newspaper Article

Reference

Author last name First initial Middle initial. Year
published Month Day. Article title. Newspaper name.
Sect Section letter or number:Page number (col Column
number).

Example

```
Richardson L. 2005 July 14. Heart attacks
    rising. The Boston Globe. Sect 1:4(col 1).
```

11.   Organization Report

Reference

[Organization name abbreviation] Organization name,
Group within organization. Year Month Day published.
Report title. Report description. Publication city (State):
Publisher. Report No.: Report number. Total pages p.

Example

```
[NEB] New England BioLabs, Phusion High-
    Fidelity. 2005 July 1. DNA Polymerase.
    Ipswitch (MA): New England Biolabs
    Publishing. 3 p.
```

Ch. 7

12.   Patent

Reference

Inventor last name First initial Middle initial, inventor; Corporate affiliation, assignee. Year Month Day issued. Patent title. Country issuing patent abbreviation Patent number.

Example

```
Zank P, inventor; BAE Systems Information and
    Electronic Systems Integration INC,
    assignees. 2002 December 10. Electric field
    sensor. US patent 315561.
```

13. Technical Report

A technical report relays research that has been funded by a sponsoring party—government, university, and organizational research reports can fall under this category.

13a.   With Author

Reference

Author last name First initial Middle initial (Organization name, City State). Year published. Report title. Publication city (State): Publisher. Total pages p. Report No.: Report number. Contract No.: Contract number. Grant No.: Grant number. Available from: Vendor name, City, State; Other identifying information.

13b.   Without Author

Reference

Organization name (Country). Year published. Report title. Publication city (State): Publisher. Total pages p. Report No.: Report number. Contract No.: Contract number. Grant No.: Grant number. Available from: Vendor name, City, State; Other identifying information.

Ch. 7

Example

```
House Permanent Select Committee on
    Intelligence and the Senate Select
    Committee on Intelligence (United States of
    America). 2002. Joint inquiry into
    intelligence community activities before
    and after the terrorist attacks of
    September 11, 2001. Washington (DC): GPO
    Access. 838 p. Report No.: 107-351.
    Available from GPO Access:
    http://www.gpoaccess.gov/serialset/
    creports/911.html.
```

14.   Unpublished Letter

You can usually cite unpublished letters and manuscripts in your reference list if they are housed at a library or are located somewhere that is accessible to the public.

Reference

Author last name First initial Middle initial. Year composed. [Letter(s) to letter recipient]. Located at: Location Building, City, State, Country.

Example

```
Atkins JL. 2005. [Letter to Andrew Durgee].
    Located at: 63 Wachusett, Worcester, MA,
    USA.
```

Ch. 7

15.   Web site

Reference

Website title [Internet]. Publication year Month Day. Publication city (State): Publisher; [updated Date updated year Month Day; cited Date cited year Month Day]. Available from: URL

Example

```
Journal of International Society of Sports
    Nutrition [Internet]. 2004-2007. Woodland
    Park (CO): International Society of Sports
    Nutrition; [cited 2007 Aug 2]. Available
    from:
    http://www.sportsnutritionsociety.org/site/
    index.php
```

Index

Chapter 4: MLA

Chapter 5: APA

Chapter 6: CMS

Chapter 7: CSE

Web-based Citation Software

Escape difficult and time-consuming reference work through SourceAid's online software. A quicker way to master writing styles rules featured in *Cite It Right*, Citation Builder organizes and creates proper citations seamlessly online.

- **Easy:** Just select a writing style and start building a bibliography, footnotes, and endnotes

- **Comprehensive:** Cite any source in MLA, APA, CMS, or CSE

- **Accessible:** Continue your research and citations at any time and place

- **Dependable:** Save work online, e-mail sources, and share research with colleagues

Try Citation Builder Pro free at http://www.sourceaid.com/go/.